100
MOST FASCINATING
PEOPLE
IN THE
BIBLE

Marie D. Jones

Publications International, Ltd.

Marie D. Jones is an ordained minister and a contributing author to many inspirational books, including *God's Promises for Teens, A Mother's Daily Prayer Book,* and *When You Lose Someone You Love: A Year of Comfort.*

ACKNOWLEDGMENTS:
All Scripture quotations are taken from the *New Revised Standard Version* (NRSV) of the Bible. Copyright © 1989, by the Division of Christian Education of the National Council of the Churches of Christ in the USA. Used by permission. All rights reserved.

COVER CREDIT: Shutterstock.com

Louis Weber, CEO
Publications International, Ltd.
7373 North Cicero Avenue
Lincolnwood, Illinois 60712

Permission is never granted for commercial purposes.

ISBN-13: 978-1-4127-1393-1
ISBN-10: 1-4127-1393-5

Manufactured in China.

8 7 6 5 4 3 2 1

Contents

The Stars of the Greatest Story Ever Told • 4

A • 5
Aaron, Abel, Abigail, Abraham, Absalom, Adam, Ahab, Amos, Ananias

B • 12
Balaam, Barnabas, Bathsheba

C • 14
Caiaphas, Cain, Caleb

D • 15
Daniel, David, Deborah, Delilah

E • 19
Elijah, Elisha, Elizabeth, Enoch, Esau, Esther, Eve, Ezekiel, Ezra

G • 26
Gideon, Goliath

H • 27
Hagar, Hannah, Herod, Herod Antipas, Hezekiah, Hosea

I • 31
Isaac, Isaiah, Ishmael

J • 33
Jacob, James, Jehoshaphat, Jeremiah, Jesus, Jethro, Jezebel, Job, John the Apostle, John the Baptist, Jonah, Jonathan, Joseph (son of Jacob), Joseph (father of Jesus), Joseph of Arimathea, Joshua, Josiah, Judah, Judas Iscariot

L • 50
Laban, Lazarus, Leah, Levi, Lot, Luke, Lydia

M • 54
Mark, Martha, Mary, Mary Magdalene, Matthew, Melchizedek, Michal, Miriam, Mordecai, Moses

N • 62
Naomi, Nathan, Nehemiah, Nicodemus, Noah

P • 65
Paul, Peter, Philemon, Philip, Pilate, Priscilla

R • 70
Rachel, Rahab, Rebekah, Reuben, Ruth

S • 73
Samson, Samuel, Sarah, Saul, Solomon, Stephen

T • 79
Tabitha, Tamar, Timothy

The Stars of the Greatest Story Ever Told

Of all the books ever written, the Holy Bible remains the best-selling and most widely read. Revered as the foundation for both the Jewish and Christian religious traditions, the Bible offers stories of hope and desperation, fear and courage, trials and triumphs, and the wisdom of the greatest prophets who ever walked the earth, including Jesus Christ.

But few readers know much about the men and women of the Bible. In *100 Most Fascinating People in the Bible*, we will meet not only those who made a huge impact on history but also those who affected their generations in more subtle ways and who made their marks, however humble and uncelebrated. We will learn who they were, what they accomplished, and what drove them—their passions and desires, challenges and obstacles, goals and missions. *100 Most Fascinating People in the Bible* profiles these intriguing characters who, collectively, told the saga of a world on the brink of spiritual transformation.

We learn about the most powerful men who ever walked the earth, as well as the most humble, whose messages of redemption and salvation gave hope to their people. They include such charismatic leaders as the lawgiver Moses, King David, and Paul the apostle to the Gentiles.

We meet dynamic women who faced huge obstacles and made choices that would have great, and sometimes grave, repercussions. They include such intriguing women as Eve, the mother of humankind; Queen Esther of Persia; and Mary, the mother of Jesus.

We discover the impact of the "bit players" and "lesser characters," those who did not hold the sway of a king or prophet, but whose roles were important parts of a bigger picture being played out over generations. They include such memorable people as Leah, the wife of Jacob; Caleb, the spy; and, of course, Mary Magdalene, the first person to see the resurrected Christ.

In this book, Bible characters are presented in alphabetical order. Each entry begins with a heading that includes the name of the person, followed by the pronunciation of that name, the meaning of that name (if known), when that person lived, and the Bible verse in which the person first appears in Scripture.

The Bible is, after all, a book about people—men and women who shaped the course of humanity, for better or for worse, and who will never be forgotten.

AARON (AIR uhn)
meaning unknown;
15 century B.C.;
Exodus 4:14

Aaron, brother of Moses and oldest son of Amram and Jochebed, came from the tribe of Levi. He married Elisheba, and they had four sons: Nadab, Abihu, Eleazar, and Ithamar. Aaron's place in the biblical story began when God commissioned Moses to release the people of Israel from slavery in Egypt. Since Moses feared that he would be an ineffective speaker for the mission, God assigned Aaron to assist his brother in freeing and leading the Hebrews.

Moses and Aaron went before the Israelites and told them of God's plan to free them; then they approached Pharaoh. The brothers worked tirelessly to bring an end to the oppression of God's covenant people. In all their efforts, the Lord directed Moses, then Moses told Aaron what to say to the people. Aaron also demonstrated God's power, and thus he helped convince Pharaoh to release the Hebrews from Egypt. On one occasion, Aaron's miraculous rod turned into a living snake that swallowed the rods of the Egyptian magicians. Another time, Aaron used his rod to strike the waters of Egypt and turn them to blood.

Aaron's most distinctive role in the Exodus events was that of high priest. When the tabernacle (the main sanctuary of worship) was established for the Israelites, Aaron became head of the priesthood and was in charge of national worship. When his authority was questioned by some, his staff budded, blossomed, and bore ripe almonds: a dramatic and colorful gesture that indicated God's choice of Aaron and his descendants as priests. Only Aaron, serving as the high priest, could enter the Holy of Holies (the most sacred section of the tabernacle) once a year to represent the people on the Day of Atonement.

Even though he was one of the most important spiritual leaders of the nation, Aaron occasionally disobeyed the Lord and demonstrated poor leadership. When Moses was on Mt. Sinai receiving God's commandments, Aaron allowed the Israelites to build an idol to worship. He even instructed them on how to make the statue. When Moses learned of what had happened in his absence, Aaron was saved from God's anger only because Moses intervened on his brother's behalf.

Later, Aaron and his sister Miriam sided together against Moses. They questioned his authority and criticized him for marrying a Cushite woman, thus challenging Moses' status as the leader of the Hebrew people. In a swift and dramatic move, God put an end to their insubordination. Miriam was stricken with leprosy and banished from the encampment. Once again, Moses begged God to show mercy, and God relented.

At the end of the wilderness journey, Aaron was kept out of the Promised Land because of the times that he had shown a lack of trust in God. Aaron died at the age of 123 on Mt. Hor, and his priestly garments were handed down to his oldest living son, Eleazar. The house of Israel mourned Aaron for 30 days.

For further study, see Exodus 4; 6–7; 17; 28–29; 32; Numbers 4; 12; 14–15; 18; 20.

❖

ABEL (AY buhl) *breath* or *vapor* or *son;* possibly *meadow;* Genesis 4:2

The story of Adam and Eve's sons, Cain and Abel, introduces the Old Testament system of sacrifices and the universal standard of faith. Though nothing was inherently wrong with Cain's farming or his offering of some of the fruits of his labors, God approved of the faith evident in Abel's animal offering because, unlike Cain, he had presented the first products of his labor, making it a "more acceptable" sacrifice (Hebrews 11:4). Ironically, the blood of Abel, who was killed by his angry and jealous brother Cain, became the prototype for future blood sacrifices, even that of Christ on the cross.

For further study, see Genesis 4:1–25; Matthew 23:34–35; Luke 11:49–52; Hebrews 11:1–4; 12:24.

❖

ABIGAIL (AB uh gayl) *my father rejoices;* 11 century B.C.; 1 Samuel 25:3

Abigail displayed the wisdom and kindness that were absent in her foolish and mean-spirited husband Nabal. When approached by King David's warriors for food rations, Nabal refused their request despite the fact that David's men had been protecting Nabal's property from warring factions in the land. Knowing this insult could mean retaliation and death for Nabal's entire household, Abigail intervened with David, begging forgiveness and offering the provisions he needed. David blessed her and accepted her offering. That night, a drunken Nabal suffered a heart attack; he died ten days later. David then married the widow Abigail and later had a child Chileab (Daniel) by her. Abigail also uttered remarkable prophecies about David's future.

For further study, see 1 Samuel 25; 30; 2 Samuel 2:2; 3:3; 1 Chronicles 3:1.

❖

ABRAHAM (AY bruh ham) *father of a multitude;* 22 century B.C.; Genesis 11:26

Abram, as he was first called, was a descendant of Noah's son Shem. He was a man of profound faith and was highly regarded wherever he went. He made his mark across the Near Eastern world nearly 4,000 years ago, from Haran in

Mesopotamia to Egypt. His story takes place primarily in the central hill country of Canaan, the land God promised to him and his descendants, who were to be the chosen people of God.

Abram was born in Ur of the Chaldees and lived there with his wife, Sarai (later called Sarah); his father, Terah; and his brothers. Abram and his nephew Lot moved their family to Haran, a trading center in the Euphrates valley. They made Haran their home, and it was there that Terah died.

When Abram was 75 years old, God made a dramatic call on his life. God told Abram to leave Haran for a new land that God would show him. He promised that he would make of Abram "a great nation" (Genesis 12:2) and vowed to bless him and give him a great name. Answering God's bidding, Abram and his entire family traveled through Shechem and Bethel into Canaan. Along the way, Abram honored the Lord, and the Lord reminded Abram that he would keep his promise to Abram and his descendants.

Walking by faith, however, was not an easy task, and Abram sometimes faltered. During this time, a severe famine came upon the region, and Abram and his household journeyed west to Egypt because food was available there. While in Egypt, Abram lied about Sarai, claiming that she was his sister. She was indeed his half-sister, but he didn't want the Egyptians to know that she was also his wife. No doubt the motive for his deception was based on the social laws of that time: In enemy territory, a husband could be murdered if someone wanted his wife. Clearly Abram felt he had to protect himself, but it almost cost him dearly.

> *Abram ... was a man of profound faith and was highly regarded wherever he went.*

Pharaoh brought Sarai into his household to add her to his harem. Abram was lavishly compensated for her with servants and livestock, but losing her would have meant that his promised blessings from God could not be realized. Fortunately for Abram, God intervened by sending plagues on the palace. Indignant when he discovered the truth about Abram and Sarai, Pharaoh returned Abram's wife to him and gave orders for the Hebrew family to take their belongings and go.

They left Egypt and returned to the hills north of Jerusalem. Soon, however, it became clear that there was not enough room or grazing ground for the large encampments of Abram and his nephew Lot. Abram resolved the problem by agreeing to let Lot move to the fruitful Jordan valley, while Abram and his camp settled in the plain of Mamre near Hebron. Once there, Abram renewed his worship and faith by setting up an altar to the Lord.

When Abram was 99 and Sarai was 90, God spoke to him once again, giving him the name Abraham and reminding him that he would be the father of many nations. The Lord instructed Abraham that he and all his male descendants should adopt circumcision as a sign to mark this covenant. Also at this time, God changed Sarai's name to Sarah and told Abraham that she would finally give birth to a son. Abraham laughed at the news but was later reminded of this promise by three strangers (angels in disguise) who visited him. Sarah, well past childbearing age, also laughed when she overheard this announcement, but in time Isaac was born to them, as God had promised.

Still, there was trouble in Abraham's clan: Some years earlier, the childless Sarah had given her Egyptian maid, Hagar, to her husband so that their household would have an heir. Hagar, the slave-girl, bore Abraham a son called Ishmael. Bitterness and jealousy grew between Sarah and Hagar over Ishmael and Isaac, and finally, Sarah told Abraham to get rid of Hagar and Ishmael. She did not want Ishmael to share Isaac's inheritance. Sarah's request troubled Abraham because of his love for his oldest son, but the Lord instructed him to do as Sarah asked and also told him that his descendants through Ishmael would be a great nation. Abraham gave Hagar and Ishmael supplies and sent them off.

Abraham's faith was most severely tested when the Lord told him to kill Isaac as a sacrificial offering. Obediently, Abraham started toward the land of Moriah on his donkey, taking with him two servants, his son Isaac, and some firewood. On the third day of the journey, they were near the mountain where the sacrifice would take place. Abraham and Isaac walked the rest of the way alone. Isaac, who was unaware of the circumstances, asked his father why there was no sacrificial lamb. Resolutely, Abraham assured Isaac that God would provide the sacrifice.

When they reached the place, Abraham built an altar, bound Isaac, laid him on the firewood, and took up the knife to kill his son. At the last moment, God intervened by providing a substitute offering. Abraham saw a ram trapped in a nearby thicket, and the animal was sacrificed instead of the boy. By agreeing to sacrifice his son, Abraham performed an extreme demonstration of his faith, and God indicated that the common pagan practice of child sacrifice would not be tolerated in the Hebrew faith. God then renewed the

> *At the last moment, God intervened by providing a substitute offering.*

promise of a blessing to Abraham and his numerous descendants.

Abraham died at the age of 175 and was buried in the Cave of Machpelah. His story marks the beginning of Israel as a people. The Bible describes his obedience to God as an outstanding example of faith (James 2:21–24).

For further study, see Genesis 11:27—25:11; Acts 13:26; Romans 4; Hebrews 7:5; 11:8; 19.

❖

ABSALOM (AB suh lahm) *father of peace;* 10 century B.C.; 2 Samuel 3:3

King David failed to punish his oldest son, Amnon, for the rape of his half-sister Tamar. So Absalom, Amnon's younger half-brother, took matters into his own hands. He lured Amnon to his death two years later on a pretense of tending sheep in the country and banqueting with family. With Amnon dead, Absalom became the crown prince and heir to David's throne, but he had to lay low for a few more years. David was furious and inconsolable in grief over the sordid acts of his children, and he refused to allow Absalom to be in his presence for some time.

Once back from exile and reinstated into David's good graces, Absalom conspired to attain his father's throne by promising justice to the common people. Absalom persuaded many to join his rebellion. This attempt to steal the hearts of the people continued for four years and became so successful that David finally had to flee Jerusalem for his life.

Absalom sealed his takeover bid by sleeping with David's concubines. However, his carefully timed rebellion soon came to a violent end. A group of David's men caught and killed the fleeing Absalom when his hair became entangled in the branches of a tree. Ironically, Absalom had always flaunted his full and luxuriant hair as a symbol of his strength and vigor.

For further study, see 2 Samuel 13–19.

❖

ADAM (AD uhm) *human being* or *humanity;* Genesis 1:26–27

On the sixth day of creation, God made humanity. He carefully shaped Adam from earthy clay, and breathed life into his body, making him a living person. He created a garden for Adam in Eden and instructed him to take care of it. God brought the animals and birds to Adam so that Adam could name them. Adam's world was pleasant and harmonious, but he was alone. God then created a woman, Eve, from Adam's rib, and Adam and Eve lived and worked together in the garden.

Earlier, God had warned Adam not to eat fruit from the tree of knowledge of good and evil. But the serpent persuaded Eve to eat the fruit; she, in turn, gave some to Adam. Immediately, they felt ashamed of their nakedness, so they covered themselves with leaves.

At the time of the evening breeze, God was walking in the garden. Feeling guilty and anxious because of what they had done, Adam and Eve hid from the Creator. God confronted them and dealt with their disobedience: He cursed the serpent to crawl forever on its belly in the dust; he told Eve she had to endure painful childbearing and to be subjected to Adam's rule; and he handed Adam over to a life of unending hardship as a farmer. Then God banished the pair from Eden so they could not eat the fruit of immortality from the tree of life. With their actions, Adam and his family brought sin and death into the world.

For further study, see Genesis 1–4; Romans 5:12–21; 1 Corinthians 15:20–49.

❖

AHAB (AY hab) *father is brother;* ruled 874–853 B.C.; 1 Kings 16:28

Ahab was politically astute, clever at foreign policy, and a financial genius. During his rule as the seventh king of Israel's northern kingdom, he fortified Israelite cities, maintained peace with the southern kingdom of Judah, and strengthened economic ties with Phoenician seaports. He was also known for his love of wealth and his showy extravagance.

Despite his successes in political and military affairs, Ahab went against the mandated religious practices of Israel by allowing and even practicing paganism. In fact, the biblical record states that Ahab did more to displease the Lord than any of the previous kings of Israel.

Ahab's marriage to Jezebel and his relationship with her father, Ethbaal, influenced his rule over Israel's religious life. Jezebel used her position as queen to champion her native Phoenician religion. Ahab agreed to build a temple with all of its pagan trappings dedicated to the false god Baal. Soon cultic practices sprang up everywhere, including promiscuous ceremonial rites dedicated to the fertility goddess, Asherah (Astarte).

Israel's most oppressive foe during Ahab's reign was Ben-hadad II of Syria. On one occasion, Ben-hadad marched his army to the gates of Samaria and besieged the city. However, Ahab surprised the enemy by launching a daytime attack. The Syrians fled, and their king narrowly escaped on horseback. Later, in a battle near Aphek, Ahab defeated Ben-hadad but agreed to spare his life in exchange for political and commercial concessions. For his lenient actions toward Ben-hadad, Ahab was told by an unknown prophet that he would lose his own life.

After this, Israel and Syria enjoyed peace for three years, probably because both nations were threatened by the imperial power of Assyria. Assyrian records indicate that Ahab supported Ben-hadad against the northern invader with chariots and men, and their common front succeeded in halting the Assyrian advance. Their alliance was short-lived, however. Once more, Ahab fought against Syria, this time with the help of Jehoshaphat, king of Judah. Even though Ahab's death in this battle was predicted by the prophet Micaiah, the king disguised himself and brazenly went into the fray. A stray arrow pierced Ahab, and by the day's end he died in a pool of his own blood. Ahab was buried in Samaria.

For further study, see 1 Kings 16:28—22:40; 2 Chronicles 18:1–34; Hosea 1:4; Micah 6:16.

❖

AMOS (AY muhs) *burden-bearer;* 8 century B.C.; Amos 1:1

Amos, a sheep farmer and a dresser of fig trees, was a pioneer among prophets. A plainspoken rustic from the small Judean village of Tekoa, he was not brought up in the class from which prophets usually came, nor was he trained in a prophetic school or guild. Nevertheless, God called upon him to perform a very difficult task: to reprimand the northern kingdom of Israel during the prosperous and peaceful reign of Jeroboam II.

Amos denounced the nation for numerous crimes against humanity, including war and other types of violence. He warned that the people would be punished for breaking and rejecting God's law. Amos thundered against Israel for luxurious self-indulgence and showing callous treatment to others, particularly the poor. He spoke against the hypocrisy of keeping up a religious front while turning "justice into poison and the fruit of righteousness into wormwood" (Amos 6:12). According to Amos, Israel had become profane, immoral, and inhuman. Its people had trampled their covenant with God.

The prophet warned that if the people did not repent, none would escape God's punishment. Amos spoke of judgment using analogies of devouring grasshoppers, a consuming fire, the builder's plumbline, summer fruit, and the smitten sanctuary. He warned of famine and drought, blight and disease, invasion and destruction. Yet his uncompromising lament was followed by an appeal to return to God, moral purity, and social justice. Amos assured the people that repentance would bring the promise of a brighter day.

However, the Israelites turned a deaf ear to the prophet, just as they did to his contemporary, Hosea. The priest Amaziah told Amos to leave Bethel, go to Judah, and preach his message there.

For further study, see Amos.

❖

ANANIAS (an uh NYE us) *protected by the Lord* or *the Lord is gracious;* A.D. 1 century; Acts 9:10

God used Ananias as an instrument to help change Saul of Tarsus—a notorious persecuter of Christians—into Paul, champion of the Christian faith. Although Ananias knew of Saul's hatred of the church, he followed God's directive to seek out Saul and welcome him by laying hands upon him. When he did so, Saul was cured of the blindness God had inflicted on him. This incident prompted Saul's conversion and began his career as the church's premier missionary.

For further study, see Acts 9:10–19; 22:12–16.

❖

BALAAM (BAY luhm) possibly *devourer;* 15 century B.C.; Numbers 22:5

Balaam, son of Beor, was a famous priest-diviner from Mesopotamia. It was believed Balaam could not only foresee coming events but could also shape their outcome by his predictions. King Balak of Moab feared the power of the Israelites as they marched toward the Promised Land. He offered to reward Balaam if he would put a curse on them while they were encamped in the plains of Moab.

Balaam declined, explaining that God would not allow him to curse a people who were "blessed" (Numbers 22:12). Balak persisted and finally persuaded the magician to visit him. On the way there, Balaam's donkey balked several times because she saw an angel and was afraid. Angered by her behavior, Balaam struck the donkey three times. The animal spoke and admonished Balaam for his actions. Balaam then saw the angel, who confronted

him. It became clear to Balaam that he could continue on this mission only if the Lord directed him.

Although Balaam's methods were not part of Israel's law, he cooperated with God as he prepared and delivered a number of oracles to the people of Israel. Instead of cursing them, he blessed the Israelites. Disappointed, the king sent Balaam home without paying him, but without daring to harm the powerful soothsayer either.

Some time later, Balaam embraced paganism, becoming involved with the Midianite nomads. Many Israelites were enticed into their idolatry and immorality, and God pronounced judgment in a holy war against the Midianites. Thousands were killed in the ensuing battle, including Balaam.

For further study see Numbers 22–24; 31; 2 Peter 2:15; Jude 11.

❖

BARNABAS (BAHR nuh buhs) *son of encouragement;* A.D. 1 century; Acts 4:36

Barnabas (also called Joseph) came from a Jewish-Cypriot priestly family and was an early Christian convert. Known as a good man, full of faith and the Holy Spirit, Barnabas personified a ministry of encouragement. His characteristic warmheartedness and spiritual insight consistently won converts and bore fruit in the Christian community.

When the early Christians emphasized sharing and stewardship, Barnabas sold his land and distributed the proceeds to needy church members. He showed the same responsive spirit when Saul (renamed Paul), the newly converted former persecuter of Christians, arrived in Jerusalem. The former archenemy of the church was given a chilly reception, but Barnabas convinced church leaders of Paul's conversion and integrity.

Barnabas chose Paul to assist him in a fruitful ministry at Antioch. They worked together for a year, encouraging disciples and evangelizing Gentiles. When the pair visited Jerusalem with contributions for famine relief, the church in Jerusalem recognized their call to Gentile missionary work.

The first missionary journey (covering 1,400 miles) resulted in the formation of many Gentile churches. On the journey, the men experienced formidable opposition, miraculous events, and even hero worship—some mistook Barnabas for the Greek god Zeus.

When the pair returned to Jerusalem, they participated in the debate over the admission of Gentiles into the church. On the next proposed journey, Paul parted company with Barnabas in a dispute over Mark (Barnabas's cousin). Barnabas took the young Mark under his wing and returned to his gospel ministry in Cyprus.

> *Barnabas sold his land and distributed the proceeds to needy church members.*

For further study, see Acts 11:22–30; 12:25—15:41; Galatians 2; Colossians 4:10.

❖

BATHSHEBA (bath SHE bah)
daughter of an oath or *daughter of abundance;* 10 century B.C.; 2 Samuel 11:2

The story of Bathsheba begins with a portrait of a beautiful woman bathing outdoors one afternoon. King David spotted her as he was walking nearby. Attracted to her, he wanted to know who she was. David discovered that her father was Eliam (or Ammiel), that her grandfather was Ahithophel (one of David's advisors), and that she was the wife of Uriah the Hittite, a soldier in David's army. Aroused by her, David sent for this married woman, and they had an affair. When Bathsheba told King David that she was pregnant with his child, David carried out a series of deceptions against Uriah to cover up his sin. These efforts finally led to Uriah's murder. After mourning her dead husband, Bathsheba married her royal lover and gave birth to their child.

After Nathan, a prophet of the Lord, confronted David about his wrongdoing, the king expressed remorse for his actions. Nevertheless, Bathsheba's tiny newborn became ill and died, and the royal household mourned. In time, David and Bathsheba had four more children: Shimea, Shobab, Nathan, and Solomon.

In David's later years, Bathsheba became a strong political force in the life of the court: With the prophet Nathan's help, she convinced David to make Solomon the next king of Israel and blocked the attempt of Adonijah, another of David's sons, to possess the throne. After David's death, she continued to exert power and influence as the mother of King Solomon.

For further study, see 2 Samuel 11–12; 1 Kings 1–2; 1 Chronicles 3:5; Matthew 1:6.

❖

CAIAPHAS (KAY uh fuhs) *meaning unknown;* A.D. 1 century; Matthew 26:3

Joseph, called Caiaphas, ruled as Jewish high priest from A.D. 18 to 36. His father-in-law, Annas, had been appointed high priest by Pilate the Roman governor. Annas and his family became the political and religious power in the Jewish community in Jerusalem.

While Caiaphas was in office, some Jewish religious leaders became restless with Jesus' growing influence, messianic claims, and alleged miracles. When Jesus raised Lazarus from the dead, the chief priests and the Pharisees were so alarmed that they called an emergency session of the Sanhedrin (the supreme court at Jerusalem). Caiaphas presided at the meeting and concluded that Jesus must die if the Jewish nation was to remain in Rome's favor. The council then devised a plan to kill Jesus. After Passover, they arrested Jesus at Gethsemane, rushed him through a preliminary trial at Annas's house, and then brought him before Caiaphas. Caiaphas tore his mantle in disbelief when Jesus admitted he was the Christ. The Sanhedrin condemned Jesus to death and delivered him to Pilate for execution.

Caiaphas continued to exert ecclesiastical influence in the early church movement. He threatened its leaders not to preach or teach, brought some apostles before his court, and presided over the trial of Stephen. Following Stephen's death, Caiaphas gave Saul authority to severely persecute all Christians under his jurisdiction.

For further study, see Matthew 26:3–5, 57–68; 27:1–2; Luke 3:2; John 11:43–57; 18; Acts 4:1–21; 6:8–14; 7:54—8:1.

❖

CAIN (KAYN) *to acquire;* Genesis 4:1

The first son of Adam and Eve, Cain was a farmer by occupation. His younger brother Abel was a herder. They both brought offerings to the Lord. Cain gave some of his produce, but Abel offered the best of what he had: the fat portions of the firstlings of his flock. God accepted Abel's offering, but rejected Cain's. Disappointed and angry, Cain was unwilling to listen to the Lord's explanations or advice about the matter. Instead, Cain took Abel out into a field and murdered him.

Later, when Cain denied killing his brother, God punished him by sending him away to become a scorned wanderer. Cain complained that the punishment was too harsh and that his life was in danger. God then put a mark on Cain so that no one would kill him.

For further study, see Genesis 4:1–24; Hebrews 11:4.

❖

CALEB (KAY leb) *dog* or *rabid;*
15 century B.C.; Numbers 13:6

Caleb served as one of the 12 tribal leaders commissioned as spies by Moses to survey the Promised Land at the end of the Exodus from Egypt. His minority report, filed along with Joshua's, advocated proceeding into Canaan as God had instructed, but the other spies convinced the Hebrews that they could not prevail against the inhabitants of Canaan. At age 85, after the Israelites had wandered in the wilderness for 40 years, faithful Caleb received his long-awaited reward: Hebron became his territory in the Promised Land.

For further study, see Numbers 13–14; 32:12; 34:19; Joshua 14:6–15; 15:13–20; 21:12; Judges 1:12–15; 1 Chronicles 4:15; 6:56.

❖

DANIEL (DAN yuhl)
God is my judge;
6 century B.C.;
Daniel 1:6

As an intellectually gifted youth from a distinguished family, Daniel was the type of child most parents and teachers would happily brag about. It's no wonder Babylonian King Nebuchadnezzar inducted him into his royal court during the time that the Hebrews lived in exile in Babylon.

Daniel and his companions Hananiah, Mishael, and Azariah were enrolled in a three-year program for courtiers. Their training was directed by Ashpenaz, the king's chief eunuch, who gave them each a Babylonian name: Daniel became Belteshazzar, and the others became Shadrach, Meshach, and Abednego, respectively. At the end of their training, the young men were brought before the king, who found Daniel and his friends not only superior to the other members of the school but also wiser than all the royal magicians and enchanters. From that point on, Daniel lived and worked at the royal court until the overthrow of the Babylonian Empire in 539 B.C.—a span of almost 70 years.

A number of years after Nebuchadnezzar's death, his successor King Belshazzar gave a great feast in the palace, and all of his household and a thousand of his nobles attended. During the merriment, members of Belshazzar's household drank wine from holy temple vessels, and libations were poured out to pagan gods. Suddenly, a mysterious hand wrote a shocking message on the palace walls. Belshazzar was dumbfounded by this and offered royal robes, gold, and prestige to anyone who could understand and interpret the strange words. Daniel, now elderly, was summoned to explain the meaning. The wise old man warned Belshazzar that by desecrating the temple vessels he had set himself against God. Daniel went on to decipher the Aramaic terms on the wall. They denoted numbers, weights, and divisions, and advised Belshazzar that his days were numbered, and that his kingdom would fall and be divided. That very night, Belshazzar was killed, and Darius the Mede subsequently conquered his kingdom.

Darius made Daniel one of the most powerful men in the kingdom. But there were those who were jealous of Daniel and sought ways to discredit him, particularly by attacking his religion. They convinced Darius to pass an edict ordering everyone to worship the king alone for a month, on penalty of being tossed to the lions. Daniel ignored the order. He continued his practice of openly praying to the God of the Hebrews three times each day. When the king was told about Daniel, he had

> *Daniel was the type of child most parents and teachers would happily brag about.*

no choice but to obey his own edict and cast Daniel into the pit with the starved lions. Yet Daniel was safe there, for "God sent his angel and shut the lions' mouths" (Daniel 6:22). The king was greatly relieved when he discovered that Daniel was unscathed. After this, Darius issued a proclamation calling for his people to honor the God of Daniel.

For further study, see Daniel; Jeremiah 25:11–12; 29:10; Revelation 1:12–16.

❖

DAVID (DAY vid) *beloved;* ruled 1003–970 B.C.; Ruth 4:17

David was the son of Jesse of Bethlehem and the great-grandson of Ruth and Boaz. The youngest of eight brothers, David was brought up to be a shepherd, and this occupation taught him compassion, patience, and courage, traits he found especially useful later in life.

When David was young, Samuel, the prophet and priest, visited Bethlehem ostensibly to make a sacrifice to the Lord. Jesse, the prosperous sheep farmer, was summoned to the ceremony along with seven of his eight sons. David was out caring for the sheep. Samuel reviewed the boys and then requested that the youngest son be brought to him. The handsome boy was presented to Samuel, and with little fanfare or ceremony, David was anointed with oil, infused with the Spirit of the Lord, and secretly marked as Israel's next king.

Subsequently, King Saul became very depressed. Ironically, David was sent to the palace to lift the king's spirits, because he was also a talented musician. David did such a good job that the king made him his armor-bearer. Whenever one of Saul's bad moods surfaced, David would play on the lyre, and Saul would feel renewed.

During this time, the Philistines and the Israelites were preparing to do battle. The Israelite forces were stationed at Elah, and Jesse sent David to the encampment with food for his warrior brothers. When he arrived, David saw a giant soldier, Goliath of Gath, parading about between enemy lines and taunting the Israelites to send out a champion to fight him. Though courageous, the soldiers were fearful of accepting his challenge.

Bolstered by his faith in God, David declared that he would meet the giant in battle. David knew he was no match for the mighty warrior, but he believed that the Lord, who had helped him protect his sheep from a lion and a bear, would also protect him from Goliath. Saul agreed to let him fight, and David went out with only a staff, a sling, and five stones to face the giant. David stunned Goliath with a stone and then used Goliath's own sword to decapitate him. Thus, David became the new champion of Israel.

After the defeat of Goliath, David remained in the king's service, and a warm friendship developed between David and Saul's son Jonathan. As David's fame and popularity grew, the king became increasingly jealous of his young rival and twice tried to kill him while he was playing music to soothe the troubled monarch. Saul also sent David on precarious, almost impossible military missions, hoping David would be killed. However, David always returned victorious, which deepened Saul's hatred for the young boy.

Matters finally came to a head when King Saul sent men to David's house to kill him. David fled to Ramah. While on the run, David used his wits, courage, and military strategy to protect himself. His guerilla force, known as the Adullam band, moved through the countryside to escape the king. Twice during this period, David had the opportunity to kill Saul, yet spared his life out of respect for the divinely appointed office that Saul held.

In a battle with the Philistines at Gilboa, Saul was killed along with his son Jonathan. David mourned greatly for the passing of the king, for his dear friend, and for the whole house of Israel.

David was finally anointed king by the men of Judah, and he established his throne in Hebron. The first two years of his reign were marked by civil war between David's supporters and the old courtiers of Saul who supported Saul's son Ishbosheth. After the tragic murder of Ishbosheth, all of Israel recognized David as their king.

David then turned his attention toward Jerusalem. He wrested this city from the Jebusites and staved off the hostile Philistines along the way. With a strong military and political hold on Jerusalem, King David decided to turn it into the capital city and the religious center of the nation. When the ark of the covenant was finally safely installed there, a relieved and thankful David danced before it.

> *Bolstered by his faith in God, David declared that he would meet the giant in battle.*

At the height of his success, however, David stumbled. During a siege against the Ammonites, David had an affair with Bathsheba, the wife of Uriah (a soldier in his army). Bathsheba became pregnant, and David ordered Uriah to be killed. The prophet Nathan condemned the king for his sin, and David repented. Still, soon after the baby was born, it became ill and died just as Nathan had warned would happen.

More strife came upon David's household. There were rape, murder, deception, and revenge among the king's children, and Absalom (popular and attractive like the young David) became estranged from his father. His resentment eventually took the form of open rebellion, and Absalom marched on Jerusalem in a surprise assault. David abandoned Jerusalem and fled for his life. He quickly assembled an army under the command of Joab and others. At Ephraim, a battle between the forces of father and son ensued, and Absalom was killed. David was heartbroken.

During his final days, David abdicated his throne in favor of his young son Solomon. On his deathbed, he told Solomon to be strong, courageous, and godly, and he instructed him in other matters as well. Then the old monarch died and was laid to rest in Jerusalem.

For further study, see 1 Samuel 16–31; 2 Samuel; 1 Kings 1–2.

❖

DEBORAH (DEB uhr uh) *bee;* 12 century B.C.; Judges 4:4

The prophet Deborah lived near the border of Benjamin and Ephraim. She was one of Israel's greatest judges, and her judgment was highly sought and trusted. Deborah was often found sitting under a palm tree between Bethel and Ramah, north of Jerusalem, and Israelites from various tribes would consult her to settle their disputes.

At that time, the Israelites had lapsed into apostasy and were oppressed in the north by Jabin the Canaanite, king of Hazor. Conveying God's instructions,

Deborah told Barak of Naphtali to gather an army on Mount Tabor against general Sisera and the army of Jabin. Even though Deborah prophesied that Sisera would die, Barak would only agree to go if Deborah went with the army. Her inspiring moral leadership was considered essential.

The Israelites overpowered the Canaanites, and Sisera fled and was killed. On that day King Jabin's domination over the Israelites in the north was broken.

For further study, see Judges 4–5.

❖

DELILAH (duh LY luh) *small or dainty;* 12 century B.C.; Judges 16:4

In the midst of turmoil between the Israelites and the Philistines, Israel's judge and mighty warrior, Samson, fell in love with Delilah, a Philistine. The Philistine rulers promised Delilah a large reward of silver if she would find out the secret of Samson's strength and then betray him. In her attempts to trick Samson, Delilah was outwitted three times. First Samson told her to bind him with seven bowstrings, then with new ropes, and finally to weave his hair with a spinning wheel. When none of these worked, Delilah pestered Samson until "he was tired to death" (Judges 16:16) and revealed that his uncut hair was the secret of his strength. Delilah had Samson's hair cut as he slept on her lap and gave him to the Philistines, who

gouged out his eyes and brought him in triumph to Gaza.

For further study, see Judges 16.

❖

ELIJAH (ee LYE juh) *the Lord is my God;* 9 century B.C.; 1 Kings 17:1

Elijah the Tishbite emerged, as if from nowhere, to become Israel's greatest miracle-worker since Moses. This great prophet from the northern kingdom of Israel was empowered by God to battle the forces of Baal, the Canaanite god of storm, rain, and fertility. Baal was acquiring a huge following among the Israelites who had forsaken their God or who were attempting to worship both God and Baal.

Elijah lived in Israel during the reign of King Ahab, whose father, King Omri, had formed an alliance with Phoenicia. Their coalition was sealed by the marriage of Ahab to Jezebel, daughter of the king of Sidon. Ahab allowed her to establish the worship of the Phoenician god Baal and his consort Asherah throughout Israel.

Against this royal pagan backdrop, Elijah, dressed only in a leather loincloth and a cloak made of hair, appeared before King Ahab to make a dramatic and harsh decree: Israel would suffer an extended drought. Before the king could order any retribution on this upstart prophet, Elijah vanished. During the drought and resulting famine, Elijah followed God's instructions and hid in a ravine next to a brook; ravens brought him meat and bread, and he drank from the brook until it dried up.

After three dry years, God told Elijah to go to Ahab and confront him about his idolatry. At that meeting, Elijah also challenged the king to a public battle of the prophets—a contest between one prophet of God and the 450 prophets of Baal on Mt. Carmel. Ahab accepted the challenge. It was decided that each side would cut up a bull, lay it on wood with no fire, and then call on their god to take the offering by fire.

The ceremony began in the morning with the appeal to Baal. By noon, after Ahab's prophets had repeatedly cried out, "O Baal, answer us!" there was still no fire. Elijah taunted them with jeers that perhaps Baal was meditating, on a journey, or sleeping. Baal's prophets became agitated, and to get the attention of their god, they slashed themselves with their swords until they were covered with blood.

When there was still no response and the time came for the afternoon sacrifice, the spectators turned their attention to Elijah. He built an altar with 12 stones (to represent the 12 tribes of Israel), laid wood and the sacrificial bull on the altar, and dug a deep trench around it. He had 12 jars of water poured over the sacrifice and the wood until the altar was saturated and the trench was overflowing. Then Elijah stood by the altar and said, "O Lord, God of Abraham, Isaac, and Israel, let it be known this day that you are God in Israel" (1 Kings 18:36).

The fire of God consumed not only the pieces of the bull but also the wood, the stones, the dust, and even the water in the trench. The people were astounded and acknowledged Elijah's God as Lord.

Instead of celebrating the victory of his God, Elijah now had to flee for his life because Queen Jezebel sought to kill him. He went into the wilderness, where the despairing prophet was fed by an angel of God and instructed to keep traveling south. Then he went to Mt. Sinai, the place where God had revealed himself to Moses and had given his Law to Israel. On this holy mountain, God again exhibited a wonderful display of nature, starting with a mighty wind that split mountains and broke rocks into pieces. Then came an earthquake and a fire, followed by total silence broken only by God speaking in a quiet voice. Elijah was instructed to select Elisha as his successor.

> *Elijah set the standard against which all future prophets and messianic figures would be measured.*

When God was ready to take Elijah to heaven, a fiery chariot took him there in a whirlwind. Elijah set the standard against which all future prophets and messianic figures would be measured. Several times in the Gospel accounts, John the Baptist and even Jesus are compared to Elijah as a way to validate their status. Elijah's significance is further established when he appears with Moses at the Transfiguration, an event that affirmed Jesus as the Son of God.

For further study, see 1 Kings 17–19, 21; 2 Kings 1–2; Malachi 4:5; Matthew 11:14; 17:1–13; 27:47–49; Mark 6:15; 8:28; 9:1–13; Luke 1:16–17; 4:25–26; 9:7–9, 18–19, 28–36; John 1:21–25; James 5:16–18.

❖

ELISHA (ee LYE shuh) *God is salvation;* 9 century B.C.; 1 Kings 19:16

Elisha was the protégé of the great prophet Elijah, who prepared his disciple to assume the role of the leading prophet of Israel. Elijah treated his successor the way a loving father would treat his son. When they parted company, Elisha asked for a double portion of Elijah's spirit, a blessing similar to the typical inheritance of a firstborn son.

Elisha's first miracle was identical to Elijah's last miracle. Beginning his ministry where Elijah left off, Elisha struck the water of the Jordan River with his inherited mantle, parting the waters to provide a dry path.

While Elijah's ministry was intense and aggressive, Elisha's was more gentle. Elijah's life was solitary; Elisha was people oriented—he often lived with groups of other prophets. Elisha showed the social aspect of his ministry when, as his second miracle, he purified the water that had been causing death, miscarriages, and crop failure in Jericho.

Elisha's healing ministry at times extended to Israel's enemies. When Naaman, a leprous Syrian army commander, came to him for a cure, Elisha instructed him to go dip himself seven times in the Jordan River. At first questioning why Israel's rivers would be any better than Syria's, Naaman finally obeyed and was healed.

Even in death, Elisha's body evidently retained some of his power to heal and restore life. Shortly after Elisha's death, a corpse was thrown into his grave, and it came to life just by touching the bones of this powerful prophet.

For further study, see 1 Kings 19:15–21; 2 Kings 2–9.

❖

ELIZABETH (ee LIZ uh beth) *God is my oath;* A.D. 1 century; Luke 1:5

Elizabeth, a descendant of Aaron, was the wife of Zechariah the priest and the mother of John the Baptist. Her husband was visited by the angel Gabriel, who said that the elderly, childless couple would soon be blessed with a son whom they should name John. Elizabeth stayed in seclusion during the first five months of her pregnancy. In her sixth month, she was visited by her cousin Mary, who was pregnant with Jesus. Elizabeth's baby jumped inside her womb when Mary entered the house. Recognizing the importance of her cousin's pregnancy, Elizabeth called Mary "the mother of my Lord" (Luke 1:43) and pronounced her blessed. When Elizabeth's own baby was born, Elizabeth named him John against the advice of her friends and neighbors.

For further study, see Luke 1.

❖

ENOCH (EE nuhk) *dedicated* or *initiated;* Genesis 5:18

What set Enoch apart from his contemporaries was not his relatively short life span—365 years as compared to Methuselah's 969—but his distinctive spirituality. Enoch "walked with God" for 300 years. That suggests a conversion experience at age 65, following the birth of Methuselah, the first of his many sons and daughters. Enoch did not die as most humans do. Instead, "God took him" (Genesis 5:24) directly into his presence. In a similar way, God would later transport Elijah to heaven.

For further study, see 2 Kings 2:10–11; Hebrews 11:5.

❖

ESAU (EE saw) *hairy* or *shaggy;* 20 century B.C.; Genesis 25:25

Before the twins Jacob and Esau were born to Rebekah and Isaac, it was pre-dicted that the elder would serve the younger. Red-haired Esau was born first, followed by Jacob, clutching his brother's heel.

Esau grew up to become a skillful hunter, while Jacob chose to work as a cultivator. On his return from a hunting trip one day, a ravenous Esau impulsively sold his birthright—the firstborn's double share of the inheritance—to Jacob in return for bread and lentil stew. When a blind and aging Isaac was preparing to give his blessing to Esau, Jacob, with the help of Rebekah, disguised himself as Esau, went before his father, and received the blessing Isaac intended for Esau.

Esau was devastated. He begged for another blessing and hated Jacob for cheating him. Esau threatened to kill Jacob, but the younger brother fled to safety. After this, Esau took his wives and settled in the land of Seir south of the Dead Sea, while Jacob and his family inhabited Canaan. Many years passed before the brothers met again. They reconciled, thanks to Esau's forgiving spirit and his willingness to accept Jacob's gift of restitution and appeasement. However, Esau became the ancestral father of the Edomites, a nation that came into repeated conflict with Jacob's descendants, the Israelites.

For further study, see Genesis 25–28; 32–33; 36; Numbers 20:18–21; Hebrews 12:16.

❖

ESTHER (ES tuhr) *star;* 5 century B.C.; Esther 2:7

To climax a six-month display of wealth and power, King Ahasuerus (Xerxes) of Persia gave a banquet on the palace grounds at Susa for all his officials and ministers. After several days of merrymaking, the king sent for his wife, Queen Vashti, to show her off. She refused to make a command appearance, which embarrassed and angered Ahasuerus. On the advice of his astrologers, he deposed Vashti and ordered a search for a new queen to replace her.

Among the beautiful young women brought to the king was a Jewish girl named Hadassah (the Hebrew word for myrtle), whose Persian name was Esther. Orphaned when she was very young, she had been adopted by her cousin, Mordecai, a devout Jew from Jerusalem who lived in exile in Susa. Esther delighted Ahasuerus, as well as all the royal court, and she was crowned queen.

Shortly after this event, Ahasuerus appointed Haman, an Agagite, as his chief minister and ordered all palace officials to show deference to him by bowing down to the grand vizier. Mordecai alone refused. As a Jew, he would not pay such an honor, as it would be tantamount to idolatry. Angered by Mordecai's refusal to prostrate himself, Haman plotted the destruction not just of Mordecai but of the entire Jewish population. Haman had the magicians cast lots to pick the day for his evil design; then he went to the king to malign the Jews. The king gave Haman his signet ring and the freedom to do as he pleased with the Jewish people.

> *Esther delighted Ahasuerus, as well as all the royal court, and she was crowned queen.*

Haman gave orders, had them published, then dispersed the royal decrees throughout the provinces. In the spring, on the 13th day of Adar, all Jews were to be killed and their possessions seized. Mordecai implored Esther to go to the king and plead for the lives of her people. It was against the law, and dangerous, for her to approach the king unbidden, but because of the urgent circumstances, she courageously agreed, declaring "…if I perish, I perish" (Esther 4:16).

The queen fasted for three days, dressed herself in regal robes, and then approached Ahasuerus. He received her, and Esther cleverly invited the king and Haman to dinner. After the meal, she invited them to a second banquet the following day. When Haman and the king were brought to Esther for the second dinner, Esther revealed her Jewish identity and told the king about Haman's plot to exterminate her people. Overcome with rage toward Haman, the king rushed out of the room. Haman, desperate for his life, violated harem law when he threw himself down on the couch beside the queen. Worse, the king found the frightened grand vizier like this when he returned from the garden and ordered Haman to be hanged.

Esther once again approached the king, this time concerning Haman's edict against the Jews. She begged the king to cancel it. The king refused since Persian law made a formal edict irrevocable, even by the king himself. Instead, Ahasuerus gave Mordecai authority to send out another decree neutralizing the first one by providing new instructions: Jews were given the right to bear arms in self-defense. And on the day Haman had appointed for their annihilation, Esther's people turned on their enemies and wiped them out. On the 14th day of Adar, the Jews celebrated not only their survival but also their amazing and complete victory. Later, Mordecai and Esther sent letters to all the Jews, establishing that the Feast of Purim should be commemorated each year to mark their deliverance.

For further study, see Esther.

❖

EVE (EEV) *life-giver;* Genesis 3:20

When God made Adam, he put him in the garden of Eden. Although a pleasant environment of birds, animals, and plants surrounded Adam, he was alone. So God set out to create a new being—a helper and partner—to provide the companionship that Adam needed. God caused Adam to sleep, removed one of his ribs, and made it into a woman. When Adam saw the woman, he recognized that she shared part of his being, and he named her Woman (Genesis 2:23). Subsequently, Adam and the woman came together in an interdependent relationship, guiltless before each other and before the Lord.

While in the idyllic garden, the clever serpent convinced the woman to eat the fruit from the tree of the knowledge of good and evil—the only restriction that God had given them. The woman gave some to Adam as well. Feeling guilty and anxious because of their disobedience, Adam and the woman covered their nakedness and hid from God. When God confronted them about what they had done, the woman told God that the serpent had tricked her. The Lord still punished her by telling her that she and all women would experience suffering in childbirth. Moreover, her mutual partnership with Adam would give way to a relationship of conflict and inequity.

Then Adam named his wife Eve "because she was the mother of all living" (Genesis 3:20). Subsequently, Eve bore many children: Cain, Abel, Seth, and other sons and daughters.

For further study, see Genesis 1:26–31; 2:18–25; 3; 4:1–2, 25; 2 Corinthians 11:3; 1 Timothy 2:13.

❖

EZEKIEL (ee ZEE kee uhl) *God strengthens;* 6 century B.C.; Ezekiel 1:3

Ezekiel was both a prophet and a priest to the Hebrew people in exile, and he ranks among the major prophets of the Old Testament, along with Isaiah, Jeremiah, and Daniel. Ezekiel lived during the greatest crisis in the Israelite history when their homeland and the temple, the center of their theocracy, were destroyed and the people were held in captivity in Babylon for 70 years. Ezekiel was among the Hebrews taken to Babylon by King Nebuchadnezzar in his second invasion of Judah in 597 B.C. His contemporary, Daniel, was taken captive in the first invasion in 605 B.C. Nebuchadnezzar invaded Judah a third time (586 B.C.), destroying the temple as well as the entire city.

Ezekiel was probably 30 years old when he was taken to a Babylonian refugee camp at Tel-Abib on the River Chebar. The only other personal notes in the Book of Ezekiel refer to his living and marital status. He had his own house and was married; evidently, Ezekiel's wife died on the eve of Jerusalem's destruction. The remainder

> *Ezekiel . . . ranks among the major prophets of the Old Testament.*

of the book deals with his warnings and prophecies to the exiled Jews.

For further study, see Ezekiel.

❖

EZRA (EZ ruh) *help* or *helper;* 5 century B.C.; Ezra 7:1

Ezra's lineage can be traced back to the priestly Hebrew tribe, the Levites, with the high priest Aaron as one of his forefathers. He was a dedicated teacher who devoted himself to the study and observance of the Mosiac Law. In 539 B.C, King Cyrus of Persia conquered Babylon and then allowed the Jews to return to Jerusalem, where they restored the city and the temple under the leadership of Nehemiah.

A small group of exiles remained in Babylon, however, either because they knew no other homeland or because they had influential positions that they were unwilling to give up. Ezra was part of this settlement and probably one of those holding an official position. He not only kept the residents on track spiritually, but he also organized a financial support group to help their comrades in Jerusalem with their rebuilding efforts. He was even able to procure support from the king himself.

After helping his homeland by proxy for many years, Ezra finally went to Jerusalem, where he began working toward his primary purpose for coming to Jerusalem: that is, to restore temple worship and observance of the Law. But Ezra soon faced the greatest moral and religious crisis of this restoration period. He met with a group of concerned leaders who explained how the Israelites had married people from the neighboring countries and adopted foreign "detestable practices" in direct violation of God's commands. Upon hearing this news of Israel's unfaithfulness, Ezra was so appalled that he tore his clothes and pulled hair from his head and beard. What followed was an anguished prayer for his people in penitence for their sins. As Ezra demonstrated his concern for his sinful nation, a group of repentant people joined him, ultimately deciding that all mixed marriages should be abandoned, thus restoring the exclusiveness of the Israelites.

In the cold and rain, the Hebrew people assembled at the square in front of the temple to hear Ezra speak. In a sermon that was short and to the point, he cited the people's sins, instructing them to confess and separate from their foreign spouses. The people were saddened by this edict but were undoubtedly prepared for the message since all but four immediately affirmed their agreement with Ezra. Though painful in its administration, Ezra's purge of foreigners was considered successful by the Israelites since it preserved their national identity and religious adherence to the Law for one more generation.

For further study, see Ezra and Nehemiah.

❖

GIDEON (GID ee uhn) *cutter* or *hewer;* 12 century B.C.; Judges 6:11

Although Gideon was one of the 12 judges before Israel became a kingdom, he did not lead or rule Israel in the same way that some of the other judges did. A meek farmer from a lesser tribe, he led an unusual military campaign to rid the Hebrews of the Midianites, a nomadic tribe that raided and plundered at will throughout Canaan.

God selected Gideon to tell the Hebrews that their plight stemmed from the way they had abandoned God in favor of idol worship. An angel instructed Gideon to destroy the temples erected to the pagan god Baal in the city of Ophrah. Fearful of reprisals from his countrymen, Gideon carried out the destruction at night in secret.

After that incident, Gideon raised an army to combat the Midianites. Lacking confidence, he asked for a sign of victory from God. That sign was to be a fleece left on the threshing room floor overnight that would gather dew on it while the floor remained dry. After receiving this sign, he still doubted and asked for another confirmation—this time that the fleece would remain dry while the floor gathered dew. This done,

God imposed a test on Gideon's faith, ordering him to reduce the size of his army to a mere 300 men so that all would know their victory came from God rather than from their military might. Facing a force of thousands, Gideon's men surrounded the Midianite camp at night and sowed confusion by simultaneously blaring trumpets and breaking pottery jars. Frightened and misled by the tumult, the Midianites fled from what they thought was a superior force, and Israel was freed from their plundering.

After the victory, Gideon was offered kingship but declined, taking instead a hoard of gold. Ironically, he fashioned the gold booty into an ephod—a pagan image that the people worshipped. God had commissioned Gideon to restore the people's faith in him, but by the end of his life, Gideon had politically elevated himself among the Hebrews while neglecting his religious obligations.

For further study, see Judges 6–8.

❖

GOLIATH (goh LY uth) *exile* or *soothsayer;* 11 century B.C.;
1 Samuel 17:4

Goliath hailed from Gath, an old Canaanite city in Judah, whose residents were called Gittites. Among them were the Anakim, warriors known for their extraordinary height. At more than nine feet tall ("six cubits and a span," 1 Samuel 17:4), Goliath stood out from the rest.

Tall and bold, Goliath paraded along the valley stream that separated the Philistine army from King Saul and his army. No Israelite dared accept Goliath's challenge of one-on-one combat to settle the conflict until the shepherd boy, David, accepted it. Relying on his faith in God, he marched into battle unprotected by armor and slew the giant with a stone from a sling. As David took the fallen Goliath's head with his own sword, the Philistines fled in panic.

For further study, see Genesis 6:4; 1 Samuel 21:9; 22:10.

❖

HAGAR (HAY gahr) *one who flees* or *flight;* 22 century B.C.; Genesis 16:1

Hagar, an Egyptian slave, served the Hebrew patriarch Abraham and his wife, Sarah. She probably became their property when Sarah entered Pharaoh's harem as a result of Abraham's cowardice and deception, and she remained with them after Pharaoh expelled them from Egypt. Hagar's life was grim, like that of any slave. Subject to her owners' every whim, Hagar's only value lay in providing labor or children.

God had promised Abraham he would father a great nation, yet Sarah was barren. Advanced in years, Sarah chose a culturally acceptable solution to infertility: She offered her slave to her husband, and Hagar conceived.

This outwardly acceptable arrangement was inwardly disastrous. Hagar's scant value rose because of her pregnancy: The child would be Abraham's firstborn. Sarah's resentment came out in harshness toward Hagar, who finally ran away into the desert. During Hagar's flight, she encountered an angel, who commanded her to return to her mistress. At the same time, the angel promised that her child would be a son, named Ishmael (meaning God hears).

> *This child was Hannah's sign that God had heard and cared.*

Several years after Hagar came back, Sarah bore a son, Isaac. As Isaac grew older, Sarah could not bear to see the elder Ishmael play with her son, so she begged Abraham to send Hagar and Ishmael away. Abraham complied with a heavy heart, but he realized that Isaac's undisputed place as his heir needed to be preserved. Despite further dire tribulations, Hagar and her son survived because of God's compassion. Ishmael's descendents became the great Arab nations.

For further study, see Genesis 15–18.

❖

HANNAH (HAN nuh) *grace;*
12 century B.C.; 1 Samuel 1:2

Imagine a woman longing for a child, taunted by her husband's second wife, and living in a culture where barrenness is considered punishment for some secret sin. That was Hannah's plight.

During her family's annual trip to worship in the sanctuary at Shiloh, she pleaded with God for a child and vowed that she would dedicate him to the Lord. Hannah was praying with such fervent emotion that Eli, the priest, accused her of drunkenness, not understanding that she was, as she put it, "pouring out my soul before the Lord."

God heard her prayer, and when the family returned home, Hannah conceived and gave birth to a son, Samuel, who later became one of Israel's greatest spiritual leaders. Hannah and her husband, Elkanah, chose a name that sounds like the Hebrew word "God has heard." This child was Hannah's sign that God had heard and cared.

Hannah kept her vow, and when the boy was weaned, she took him to the sanctuary to live with Eli.

For further study, see 1 Samuel 1–3; Psalm 113; Luke 1:46–56.

❖

HEROD (HAIR uhd) the Great; ruled 37–4 B.C.; Matthew 2:1

Twenty-five years after the Roman army destroyed Jerusalem in 63 B.C., Herod the Great reconstructed its various pieces into a kingdom under his domain. He skillfully served Rome while appeasing his Jewish subjects. But his main legacy was architectural, not political, outdoing even Solomon at his peak. Herod the Great reconstructed many public buildings, including the Jerusalem temple that Jesus visited and that the Romans later destroyed. Despite his greatness, Herod was insanely jealous of another "king of the Jews" born in Bethlehem. In an act of cruel barbarism, he ordered the murder of all male babies born around the same time as Christ. However, Jesus and his family fled to safety in Egypt.

For further study, see Matthew 2:1–23; Luke 1:5.

❖

HEROD ANTIPAS (HAIR uhd AN ti puhs) *sprung from a hero;* ruled 4 B.C. to A.D. 39; Matthew 14:1

The ruler of Galilee and Perea during the ministries of Jesus and John the Baptist, Herod Antipas is best remembered for the role he played in their arrests and deaths.

John the Baptist lost his life after condemning Herod Antipas for violating the law by adulterously marrying his brother's wife, Herodias, while his brother was still alive. Herodias had John imprisoned for this affront, but she wanted further punishment for him. When an impulsive Antipas promised Herodias's daughter Salome anything she wanted in appreciation for pleasing him with her dancing, Salome (prompted by her mother) demanded, "Give me the head of John the Baptist here on a platter" (Matthew 14:8). And so it was done.

Herod Antipas also played a role in the arrest, mockery, and eventual execution of Jesus. At first a secret admirer of Jesus, Antipas was eager to see the Galilean perform miracles. But Antipas turned against him when Jesus refused to perform on command. Neither defending nor condemning him, Antipas left the decision of Jesus' fate up to Pontius Pilate.

In A.D. 39, Antipas lost his power to Herod Agrippa I and spent his remaining years in exile.

For further study, see Matthew 14:1–12; Mark 6:14–29; Luke 3:19–20; 8:3; 9:7–9; 13:31–35; 23:6–12; Acts 4:26–27; 13:1.

❖

HEZEKIAH (HEZ uh KYE uh) *the Lord is my strength;* ruled 729–686 B.C.; 2 Kings 16:20

When Hezekiah took the throne of Judah, he was only 25, Assyrian invaders were threatening the borders, and the nation was in spiritual and economic ruin. Yet, Hezekiah's reign is a spot of light in a mostly dark period of Jewish history.

When Israel split into separate Hebrew nations, Israel and Judah, neither country followed God. Rulers and common people alike worshipped idols, warred among themselves, and became like the surrounding pagan nations. From the day Jeroboam worshipped a golden calf in Israel until Hezekiah's own father, Ahaz, practiced child sacrifice in Judah, nearly every generation ignored the ways of God. Hezekiah and the prophet Isaiah stood virtually alone, examples of the few faithful Jews God had promised would always remain.

Hezekiah wanted to be a king like David. He understood how God abhorred the worship of idols, so he struck down altars and destroyed sites of idol worship. He pulled down the sacred pole of the Canaanite goddess Asherah and ground it to dust. Then Hezekiah rebuilt the temple, which had been neglected for generations. He fortified Jerusalem, rebuilding walls, towers, and battlements. In a feat of ambitious engineering, he commissioned the digging of a tunnel to connect the spring outside the city walls with a reservoir inside. The 600-yard tunnel gave the city a direct water supply and lessened its vulnerability to siege.

During the first years of Hezekiah's reign, Israel was conquered by Assyria. A few years later, the Assyrians tried to annex Judah to their kingdom as well. Faced with such a threat, Hezekiah aligned himself with other nations to fight the Assyrian onslaught. However, just as they had taken Israel, the Assyrians claimed city after city in Judah. Their military might overcame Judah's armies, and finally, Hezekiah himself was placed under house arrest.

> *Hezekiah is known more for his faith in God than his wisdom as a ruler.*

Hezekiah's submission and defeat was not enough for the Assyrian king. The final trophy for King Sennacherib was the heart of Judah—its capital, Jerusalem. He sent nearly 200,000 soldiers to the city gates with a demand of surrender, knowing Judah could not fight such an army. Sennacherib sent a message mocking the God of the Jews. His envoys called out to the people on Jerusalem's walls, saying they were fools to follow Hezekiah, and greater fools to think their God would save them.

Yet God spoke to the prophet Isaiah, saying Sennacherib would never enter Jerusalem but would return to die by the sword in his own land. The next morning, 185,000 Assyrian soldiers were dead, killed by an angel of the Lord. By the time the terrified survivors reached home, King Sennacherib was battling invading armies on all fronts. The king finally fled to Nineveh, where he was murdered with a sword.

Some years later, when Hezekiah was near death, the prophet Isaiah told him to set his house in order and prepare to die. At this, Hezekiah turned his face to the wall and wept. He prayed, asking God to remember how he had walked before God in faithfulness "with a whole heart" and tried to do right all his life. God heard Hezekiah's prayer. He stopped Isaiah in the middle of the courtyard and said, "Go and say to Hezekiah...I have heard your prayer" (Isaiah 38:5).

God promised Judah's king 15 more years of life and protection from the Assyrians for Jerusalem. When Isaiah told him these things, Hezekiah asked for a sign that the promises would happen. Isaiah cried out to the Lord, and when God made the shadow on the sundial move backward "ten intervals," there was no doubt. Hezekiah recovered and went to the temple on the third day. He lived those 15 years, and during that time, invaders did not take the city of Jerusalem.

King Hezekiah is known more for his faith in the Lord than his wisdom as a ruler. In the end, political ambition and military mistakes were his undoing. While he believed in the God of Israel, he did not always follow the counsel of God's prophet, Isaiah. Perhaps seeking peaceful coexistence, he made alliances with Babylon and revealed the secret wealth of his kingdom to their ambassadors.

The king continued offers of friendship even after Isaiah received a prophetic vision warning that an alliance with Babylon would be the beginning of Judah's destruction. Hezekiah ignored the warning, trading peace and prosperity in his own time for the lives of his descendants. Still, when Hezekiah died, all Judah honored him.

For further study, see 2 Kings 18–20; 2 Chronicles 29–32; Isaiah 1:1; 36–39; Jeremiah 26:18–19; Hosea 1:1; Micah 1:1.

❖

HOSEA (ho ZAY uh) *the Lord has saved;* 8 century B.C.; Hosea 1:1

The Bible is filled with images of marriage: God is called a husband to widows; Jesus is the bridegroom, and the church is his bride. In the first three chapters of the Book of Hosea, however, one marriage symbolizes the history of God's love for Israel and Israel's betrayal of that love.

Hosea was an Israelite prophet who was told by God to marry a prostitute named Gomer. He offered her his love, but she continued to sell herself to any man with money.

Gomer repeatedly betrayed Hosea with many lovers. In the same way, the ancient Israelites often betrayed their covenant with God, worshipping at festivals, pagan temples, and roadside altars. As Gomer ran after her lovers, Israel ran after the idols and gods of every surrounding nation.

For further study, see Hosea.

❖

ISAAC (I zak) *laughing* or *he laughed;* 21 century B.C.; Genesis 17:19

Isaac was the "child of promise." God promised a 99-year-old man and his 90-year-old wife a child. Although at first the couple laughed at the prospect, Isaac was born as Abraham's heir and the father of the next generation of God's chosen people.

Isaac married Rebekah, a relative of his father, instead of one of the idol-worshipping Canaanite women who lived nearby. He put his faith in God even when he and his wife were unable to conceive a child at first, and in the end they were given twin sons, the younger being Jacob, the third patriarch of the Jewish nation.

For further study, see Genesis 15:1–6; 16–18; 21–29; Galatians 4:28; Romans 9:6–13.

❖

ISAIAH (I ZAY uh) *the Lord is salvation;* 8 century B.C.; 2 Kings 19:2

Isaiah is among the greatest of ancient Israel's prophets. He was a scholar, statesman, and poet, and throughout his 50 years of prophetic ministry in Israel, he confronted evil, foretold future events, communicated God's will to rulers and citizens, and trumpeted an ongoing call to return to the ways of God.

At age 25, Isaiah had a vision in which God asked for a prophet willing to speak God's word. When Isaiah answered, "Here am I. Send me!" (Isa 6:8), his life's direction was set in motion. His ministry spanned the reigns of four kings, beginning at the death of King Uzziah and lasting through the reigns of Jotham, Ahaz, and Hezekiah.

Isaiah lived in a time of political and spiritual upheaval. Israel had split into the separate monarchies of northern Israel and southern Judah, Assyrian and Egyptian military assaults kept every small nation in fear, and few God-fearing kings had sat on Judah's throne. Amid this confusion, Isaiah was called to speak for God.

Isaiah lived all his recorded life in Jerusalem. His love for the city and his unveiled understanding of its failings are apparent in his writings. He called Jerusalem both a "faithful city" and a "harlot." Prophets Micah and Amos spoke about these social justice issues, but they were rural farmers and may have been poor themselves. Isaiah spoke to the wealthy as a peer, and his words of condemnation were perhaps harsher because of it.

Isaiah may be best known for his prophecies about the Messiah. Jews in every era have waited and hoped for God's promised Savior, and Christians consider many chapters of the Book of Isaiah to be direct prophecies pointing to Jesus.

For further study, see 2 Kings 19:1–7; Isaiah.

❖

ISHMAEL (ISH may uhl) *God heard;* 22 century B.C.; Genesis 16:11

Ishmael grew up as Abraham's eldest son and heir. At 13, he was circumcised, marking him as a participant in Abraham's covenant with God. But then, angels told Abraham that the promise of his great nation was to be fulfilled not through Ishmael but through a child conceived by Sarah. When this son, Isaac, was born, Ishmael became dispossessed. Sarah asked that Ishmael be sent away, for he posed a threat to Isaac's inheritance. Abraham was reluctant to banish his son, but God instructed him to do so, reassuring Abraham that from Ishmael would come another great nation.

Wandering in the wilderness, Ishmael and his mother, Hagar, almost died of thirst. An angel directed them to a well, and there they settled. Ishmael married and established a clan of desert dwellers considered to be the ancestors of today's Arab nations.

For further study, see Genesis 16–17.

❖

JACOB (JAY kuhb) *supplanter;* **20 century** B.C.; **Genesis 25:26**
Jacob's birth was a metaphor for his life. In the womb, he struggled with his twin brother, Esau, and was born clutching the elder Esau's heel. While his name means supplanter, a more literal, albeit less polite, meaning is "grabber"; and grab he did.

Jacob and Esau's struggle for primacy in the womb continued throughout their lives, aggravated by their parents' favoritism, for Rebekah favored Jacob while Isaac favored Esau. In this struggle, Jacob became manipulative and deceitful; he grabbed everything Esau had. Because Esau was firstborn, Esau received the birthright. In the ancient Hebrew culture this traditionally meant twice the inheritance of money and property, headship of the family, and a social and spiritual position of leadership. Jacob was not content with one third of the inheritance and a subservient position, so he schemed to take his brother's birthright.

Jacob found his opportunity one day when Esau was returning from a hunting trip famished. The wily Jacob offered his brother food in exchange for his birthright, and Esau accepted. Later, Jacob added to this deception by stealing the blessing that Isaac intended for Esau. The paternal blessing of children was a common Middle Eastern custom and conveyed more than good wishes; it was a stamp of approval and transfer of authority. Isaac had reserved this blessing for Esau, but because Isaac was old and nearly blind, Jacob and his mother were able to trick him. At Rebekah's suggestion, Jacob covered his arms and neck with lamb's wool, disguising himself as his hairy older brother. Isaac was deceived and gave his blessing to Jacob instead of Esau.

When Esau discovered that Jacob had again grabbed something intended for him, he was enraged and vowed to kill his brother. Rebekah was afraid, and under the guise of sending him to seek a wife from her extended family, she sent Jacob north, to her homeland. About

60 miles from home, Jacob had a dream in which God stretched a ladder between heaven and earth. God stood at the top, assuring Jacob that the promise Abraham received would be made good for him, as Abraham's descendant. When Jacob woke, he poured oil over the stone under his head to mark the place of God's presence.

In Paddanaram, Rebekah's birthplace, Jacob met his match. In a show of hospitality common to the times, his uncle Laban hosted Jacob for a month. Then, he asked what wages Jacob might require to stay and work with Laban's herds. Jacob had come to love Rachel, and said, "I will serve you seven years for your younger daughter, Rachel." Laban agreed.

After seven years, the time came for Jacob and Rachel's marriage, and Laban's true nature was revealed. Jacob took his veiled bride into a dark tent to consummate the marriage. However, the morning sun showed that Laban had veiled Leah, Rachel's older sister, and Jacob had married her instead. Laban did eventually agree that Jacob could marry Rachel after the feast for Leah ended; however, he required seven more years of labor as a price for her.

Finally, Jacob, with his large family, returned to his homeland, and as he came near, he sent gifts ahead, hoping to soften Esau's anger. That night, Jacob

During the night, an angel in human form wrestled with [Jacob].

sent everyone to the far side of the river and stayed alone, in case Esau should come. During the night, an angel in human form wrestled with him. At daybreak the angel pulled away, but despite fatigue and a dislocated hip, Jacob clung to him, saying he would not let go without the angel's blessing. The angel asked Jacob's name and said, "You shall no longer be called Jacob, but Israel," a name meaning "One who strives with God." Esau then met his brother in welcome and forgiveness. Jacob settled in Canaan while Esau remained across the Jordan River in Seir.

For further study, see Genesis 26–35; 37:18–28; 38–47; Romans 9:13.

❖

JAMES (JAYMZ) *supplanter*, A.D. 1 century; Matthew 13:55

Many scholars consider James, the first leader of the Jerusalem church, to be the brother of Jesus. He was known for wisdom and integrity, qualities that are amply illustrated in the Epistle of James, in which he wrote about righteous behavior and good works as evidence of faith.

James was called "the Just," perhaps to honor his leadership of the early Church. In his epistle, he humbly called himself only "a servant of God and of the Lord Jesus Christ," placing his brother above himself. The Jewish historian Josephus recorded James's death by stoning in A.D. 62.

For further study, see James; 1 Corinthians 15:7; Acts 21:17–26.

❖

JEHOSHAPHAT (juh HAHSH uh fat) *the Lord has judged;* ruled 872–848 B.C.; 1 Kings 15:24

Jehoshaphat, the fourth king of Judah, learned a difficult lesson from his father and predecessor, King Asa. Although Asa followed God early in his reign, his pride later prompted him to reject God's judgment. Following the flattering words of false prophets rather than the will of the Lord, Asa fell ill and died.

When Jehoshaphat assumed the throne, he became one of the few God-fearing kings of Judah or Israel. In addition to destroying many sites of idol worship and restoring the temple, he personally appointed judges and set the Law of Moses as their standard.

During Jehoshaphat's reign, three nations combined to invade Judah. When messengers reported approaching armies, Jehoshaphat's response was unlike that of any of Judah's kings either before or after him. He assembled the entire nation to pray. Jehoshaphat himself prayed, "O our God...we are powerless against this great multitude....We do not know what to do, but our eyes are on you" (2 Chronicles 20:12).

Jehoshaphat's army went out to meet the invaders and found their corpses strewn across a valley; the invading armies had turned on each other and destroyed themselves. Jehoshaphat's army returned to Jerusalem singing praise to God for his protection. Jehoshaphat reigned for 25 years in Jerusalem.

For further study, see 1 Kings 22:1–50; 2 Chronicles 17–20.

❖

JEREMIAH (JAIR uh MYE uh) *the Lord establishes* or *the Lord is exalted;* 7–6 century B.C.; 2 Chronicles 35:25

Jeremiah was scarcely out of childhood, age 12 or 13, when God called him to be a prophet. Jeremiah heard the words, "Before I formed you in the womb I knew you, and before you were born I consecrated you." When Jeremiah protested that he was only a boy, God replied, "Now I have put my words in your mouth" (Jeremiah 1:5, 9).

When King Josiah died in battle with the Egyptians, Jeremiah wept because the king had been faithful to the Lord. For the next 40 years, Jeremiah watched unfaithful king after unfaithful king take Judah's throne. When the Hebrews were exiled to Babylon, Jeremiah prophesied that their exile would last 70 years, after which they would return to their own land.

Jeremiah himself had not been taken to Babylon. Evidently his fame had spread, because the Babylonian king commanded that he be treated well. He was allowed to stay in Judah with

Gedaliah, the interim governor. But Gedaliah was assassinated, and so Jeremiah had to flee to Egypt. He remained there, and continued to prophesy. Little is recorded of those years.

Jeremiah was known for his dramatic prophecies and unusual life. For example, God told him not to marry, as a symbol of Judah's hopeless future. Jeremiah's harsh warnings contrasted with his sensitive spirit. When rejected and hounded by the very kings he hoped would turn to God, he cried out in hurt and anguish.

Jeremiah was an example of amazing perseverance in spite of danger and rejection. He was direct and confrontational; he once cut off his hair to illustrate mourning and smashed a clay pot to show how Judah would be shattered. He boldly described Judah and Israel as whores, who "refuse to be ashamed" (Jeremiah 3:3). However, not all of Jeremiah's prophetic words were condemning; he also spoke of God's forgiveness with words like, "Return, O faithless children, I will heal your faithlessness" (Jeremiah 3:22).

For further study, see 2 Chronicles 35–36; Jeremiah; Matthew 2:17–18; 27:3–10.

❖

JESUS (JEE zuhs) *salvation;* A.D. 1 century; Matthew 1:1

Jesus was a common name among Jews during the period of Roman occupation. But Jesus of Nazareth was no common man. He is the historical figure whom Christians believe to be the Son of God incarnate. The most common title ascribed to Jesus is Christ, which is Greek for Messiah, meaning "anointed one."

To Christians, Jesus is God's promised Savior. Scriptures say the birth of this Savior was remarkably humble in its circumstances yet divinely orchestrated in its conception. Apart from the description of his birth and circumcision, the biblical story of Jesus' first 12 years is silent. In his Gospel account, Luke records that at age 12, Jesus attended his first Passover feast in Jerusalem with his family. At the temple, Jesus listened to the rabbis and then amazed all of them with his own unique wisdom and understanding.

It was another 18 years before Jesus went public with his teachings. Jesus' public ministry began in earnest when his cousin, John the Baptist, saw him and announced: "Here is the Lamb of God who takes away the sins of the world!" (John 1:29). Jesus submitted to John's baptism of repentance on behalf of all Israel. As Jesus rose from the Jordan River, "the Holy Spirit descended on him in bodily form like a dove" (Luke 3:22). Jesus then retreated to the desert where Satan tempted him for 40 days but failed.

As reported in four Gospel accounts, many personal and powerful encounters characterized Jesus' earthly ministry as he traveled throughout cities of Galilee, proclaiming the kingdom of God. Of the many people he met in the course of his travels around Galilee, Jesus chose 12 men in particular to be his closest disciples. All Jesus expected from these men was their companionship, their obedience to his teachings, and their commitment to follow his example.

Jesus frequently used human and earthly analogies to express spiritual or eternal concepts. He often taught moral issues and spoke of humanity's relationship to God by using parables—brief narratives and analogies that illustrate a spiritual truth. However, the Bible portrays Jesus as more than just a good teacher or great ethicist. In addition to Jesus' memorable sayings, Scripture has preserved numerous accounts of miracles performed by Jesus, supporting the idea that he is indeed the Son of God. Stories of Jesus making the blind see and the mute speak, causing the deaf to hear and the paralyzed to walk, feeding the masses with a few loaves of bread, curing diseases, and even raising the dead—all these are meant to verify Jesus' claims of divinity.

Meanwhile, the Sanhedrin, the Jewish high council, was disturbed that Jesus claimed to be the Son of God. Some of them were also afraid that

> *Scripture has preserved numerous accounts of miracles performed by Jesus, supporting the idea that he is indeed the Son of God.*

Jesus' popularity would turn the Romans against the Jewish nation. Whenever Jesus taught or healed, these leaders sought a way to stop him. Led by Caiaphas, the high priest, they finally met to plan his demise.

Their plan culminated before the Passover feast in Jerusalem a few days after Jesus had entered the city on a donkey thronged by people shouting "Hosanna!" During that week of Passover, Jesus ate one last supper with his disciples and prayed in the Garden of Gethsemane, where he was betrayed by Judas Iscariot (one of Jesus' original 12 disciples). The Sanhedrin convened late at night in special session and convicted Jesus of blasphemy. Jesus' friends on the council, such as Nicodemus and Joseph of Arimathea, were excluded from the session. Since the Sanhedrin was not allowed to sentence anyone to death, the conspirators took him to Pontius Pilate, the Roman governor of Judea.

Pilate questioned Jesus in the Praetorium, not about blasphemy but about possible treason stemming from the itinerant preacher's claim of being King of the Jews. When Jesus explained that his kingdom was not of this world, Pilate announced to the crowd that he could find no fault in him. Thinking he could rid himself of any lingering liability, Pilate passed off Jesus to King Herod, who only mocked him and sent him back to Pilate.

In the Jewish nation, a prisoner of the people's choice was customarily released each year during Passover. Pilate offered to release Jesus as the annual appeasement. But a mob inflamed by the conspirators insisted that he instead release Barabbas, a notorious assassin. When Pilate asked what he should do then with Jesus, the crowd shouted, "Crucify him! Crucify him!" With Jesus refusing to defend himself before Pilate and the crowd growing angrier and more insistent, Pilate finally washed his hands of the matter. He handed Jesus over to die an agonizing death on a Roman cross, between two common thieves.

After Jesus died, Joseph of Arimathea and Nicodemus took his body from the cross, prepared it for burial, and placed it in Joseph's own unused tomb. A couple of days later, three devoted followers of Jesus went to his tomb to anoint his body, but these women found the tomb empty. An angel at the entrance to the tomb met them and told them that Jesus had risen from the dead.

Jesus' disciples and more than 500 others over the span of the next 40 days subsequently met the living Savior until they witnessed his ascension into heaven.

For further study, see Matthew, Mark, Luke, and John; other New Testament books offer reflections on Jesus' significance to humanity.

❖

JETHRO (JETH roh) *excellence;* 15 century B.C.; Exodus 3:1

As a young man, Moses killed an Egyptian and fled to the land of Midian on the Sinai Peninsula. There he met a tribe, the Kenites, who were shepherds in that region. Moses married Zipporah, the daughter of a wise Midianite priest named Jethro, and tended Jethro's sheep until God ordered him to return to Egypt. When Moses led the Israelites out of Egypt, Jethro brought Zipporah and her sons to the Israelites' camp. Upon hearing the amazing way God had saved Israel from Pharaoh, Jethro said, "Now I know that the Lord is greater than all gods" (Exodus 18:11). While Jethro stayed with the Israelites, he helped Moses by showing him how to delegate responsibility by appointing judges instead of governing alone.

For further study, see Exodus 2:11—3:12; 18.

❖

JEZEBEL (JEZ uh bel) *meaning unknown;* 9 century B.C.; 1 Kings 16:31

Jezebel, a Phoenician princess, was married to King Ahab of Israel. During their marriage, she continued to worship Baal, the fertility god of her people. Ahab not only joined her, but he also built a temple for Baal and erected a pole for worship of the goddess Asherah, Baal's consort. Jezebel actively promoted Baal worship throughout the realm, using money from the treasury to pay 950 prophets of Baal and Asherah. She may even have been a priestess of Baal herself. Finally, to secure the stamp of her pagan god upon Israel, Jezebel ordered the Hebrew prophets killed.

Jezebel was noted for her cruelty. She even arranged the execution of an innocent man, Naboth, to acquire his land for Ahab's garden. In prophecy, Elijah declared that dogs would eat her because of her wickedness. Jezebel died during a rebellion. When her body was found, only the skull, feet, and the palms of her hands remained.

For further study, see 1 Kings 16:31–33; 18:20–40; 19:1–10; 21:1–28; 2 Kings 9:30–37.

❖

JOB (JOHB) *meaning unknown;* Job 1:1

The Book of Job records the story of a wealthy, pious man whose good life turned to ashes because God allowed Satan to test Job's faith. Both Jewish and Christian traditions have long honored Job for his faith and spiritual endurance.

> *Both Jewish and Christian traditions have long honored Job for his faith and spiritual endurance.*

Job lived in the "land of Uz." Because the names of Job's three friends mentioned in the story were Edomite in origin, Uz may have been near or in Edom. Some Hebrew traditions place Job in Hauran, a fertile area east of the Jordan River. And because Job's lifespan is listed as 140 years, he may have lived during the time of Abraham when some people lived about that many years according to the Bible.

Job's tale begins in heaven when God praised him for his outstanding faith. Satan, called "the accuser" in the biblical record, dismissed Job's faith, saying Job was righteous only because God had blessed and protected him. Satan proposed that if Job lost his wealth and loving family, Job would curse God. So God gave Satan the freedom to destroy everything of Job's except his life.

Within one day, nomadic raiders stole Job's herds and his ten children died. Later Job was struck with a repulsive disease that left him covered with infected sores. Job now sat on an ash heap, scraping his sores with a bit of broken pottery. His unsympathetic wife looked at the destruction of their lives and told Job to "curse God and die."

Job was then joined by three friends: Eliphaz, Bildad, and Zophar. In this segment of the Book of Job, God's nature is examined alongside the question of human suffering and God's will. At the end of Job's dialogue with his friends, "out of the whirlwind," God finally answered Job's complaints, "Who is this that darkens counsel by words without knowledge?" Then, both challenging and demonstrating his own absolute power, God asked where Job was when the earth was created.

Job's encounter with the Almighty sheds light on his faulty assumption that humans could hold God accountable for his actions. God's oft-repeated question "Where were you?" asked, in effect, "Have you earned the right to question me?" Job said, "I lay my hand on my mouth...I have uttered what I did not understand, things too wonderful for me, which I did not know." Once, he admitted he had only heard about God and had thought he understood what he heard. Now, however, he had seen and experienced God firsthand and said, "I repent in dust and ashes." In the end, Job's fortune and family were restored twofold, as a blessing from the Lord for his faithfulness.

For further study, see Job; Ezekiel 14:14; James 5:11.

❖

JOHN THE APOSTLE; A.D. 1 century; Matthew 4:21

The New Testament often refers to Peter, James, and John as the three who made up Jesus' inner circle. Jesus often spoke with them apart from the rest of the apostles, and only these three viewed Jesus' Transfiguration and stayed closest with him in the garden of Gethsemane.

John himself grew up in Bethsaida, learning the fishing trade from his father, Zebedee. According to Luke's Gospel, John and James were business partners with another pair of brothers, Simon (called Peter) and Andrew. One day Jesus saw the four men fishing and called out to them, "Follow me and I will make you fish for people." Luke records that they left everything—boats, equipment, and family—and followed him. James and John were impetuous, spirited men, as rugged as the Galilean hills. They were called Boanerges, or "sons of thunder."

Nevertheless, John was also deeply sensitive. On one occasion, Jesus, James, and John went to the home of the Jewish leader Jairus, because the man's daughter had died. Though Jesus would later revive the girl, her tragic death obviously touched John, because he wept along with the mourners.

While Jesus died on the cross, John stood with Mary, Jesus' mother. He watched his Lord suffer terribly, all of which he recorded in his own Gospel account. Jesus clearly noted John's loyalty and compassion by asking John to take care of his mother, which John did for the rest of her life.

After the death and resurrection of Jesus, John often traveled with Peter, preaching, healing, and teaching the new faith. The two men were arrested, imprisoned, beaten, and interrogated by the temple leaders. An angel once released them from prison while the doors remained locked and the guards stood outside.

John remained in Jerusalem, as one of the leaders of the new Church. The New Testament also credits him with authorship of three epistles and equates him with the John who was exiled to the island of Patmos, where he recorded a vision now known as the Book of Revelation.

For further study, see Mark 1:19–20; 3:17; 10:37; Luke 9:40–54; John 1:35–37; Acts 4:1–23; 8:14–25; 12:1–2; Galatians 2:9; Revelation 1–2.

❖

JOHN THE BAPTIST; A.D. 1 century; Matthew 3:1

The life of John the Baptist was radical from its beginning. His parents, Elizabeth and Zechariah, were elderly and childless. When the angel Gabriel announced John's conception, his father doubted the angel's words and was struck dumb as punishment. After John was born, Zechariah's first words were an amazing prophecy about his son. Zechariah said God had chosen the child as a prophet of the Most High to prepare the way for the Lord, preaching salvation through forgiveness of sins.

> *[Jesus asked] John to take care of his mother, which John did for the rest of her life.*

John was related to Jesus, as his mother was cousin or close kin to Mary, Jesus' mother. He was raised in an orthodox Jewish home, for both parents came from priestly families where life centered around learning the Torah and religious and ethnic traditions of family, faith, and congregation. In adulthood, John lived in the Judean hills, a hot wasteland east of the Jordan River. He wore camel hair and leather, living a rustic life in this wilderness, where God first called him to be a prophet. John the Baptist preached throughout the countryside about changed hearts and turning from sin, using baptism as a symbol of cleansing and forgiveness. The words "the kingdom of God is at hand" became a symbol of his ministry. Clearly, John saw something, or someone, on the horizon.

This odd-looking desert "wild man" attracted an audience of thousands. Some of his listeners became followers, learning from his preaching and asking to be baptized. They were impressed with his spirited preaching and the fact that he challenged the ritualism and legalism of the religious establishment of his day. Even Jesus came to the Jordan to be baptized.

John's reputation grew, until people began to ask if he might be the Messiah. John answered in true character. The

Messiah would come, "to baptize with the Holy Spirit and fire," he said. "But I am not worthy to carry his sandals" (Matthew 3:11). Later, John instructed his disciples to follow Jesus, insisting that his own influence had to decrease in order that Jesus' might increase.

John's uncompromising nature eventually brought him trouble. When Herod Antipas, Rome's appointed ruler in Israel, married his brother's wife Herodias, John the Baptist condemned both of them publicly. Herodias angrily demanded that her husband imprison this Jewish preacher. When imprisoning John did not satisfy her desire for revenge, she arranged for his death. At a party for Herod's birthday, Herodias's daughter Salome danced erotically for the guests. Scripture records that Salome so enticed Herod that he offered her anything she wished. At her mother's direction, Salome demanded, and received, the head of John the Baptist on a platter.

For thousands of years, the Jewish people had waited for the Messiah. Many Old Testament prophecies foretold a Savior, but one in particular, found in Malachi 4:5, promised that a great prophet, like Elijah, would come before the Messiah to prepare the people. Matthew stated that John the Baptist fulfilled this ancient prophecy by preparing Israel for the coming of Jesus.

For further study, see Matthew 3:1–17; 11:2–19; 21:31–32; Mark 1:1–11; 6:14–29; Luke 1:5–25, 39–80; 7:18–35; Acts 1:6–9; 19:1–7.

❖

JONAH (JOH nuh) *dove;* 8 century B.C.; 2 Kings 14:25

Jonah's mission was to bring God's word of judgment to one of Israel's most violent enemies, Assyria. The Book of Jonah begins, "Now the word of the Lord came to Jonah, son of Amittai, saying, 'Go at once to Nineveh...and cry out against it; for their wickedness has come up before me'" (Jonah 1:1–2). Jonah promptly ran in the opposite direction. Nineveh was a prominent Assyrian city, the capital of the empire noted for ferocity and cruelty in battle; their troops would sweep through villages, killing even infants with a viciousness that left neighboring nations trembling.

Jonah went to Joppa, on the coast, and boarded a ship bound for Tarshish, probably a city on the western coast of the Mediterranean. During the voyage, a storm nearly broke the ship apart. In the face of certain death, the sailors cried out, each to his own god. In ancient times, most tragedies were considered punishment for sin. With this perspective, the sailors cast lots to determine the guilty party, and the lot fell to Jonah. Jonah said they must throw him into the sea because his disobedience was the reason for the storm. Finally, when the storm increased so they could no longer control the ship, the men reluctantly threw him overboard. A great fish swallowed Jonah, and during the three days and nights spent in its belly, Jonah thanked the Lord for having saved him from drowning in the sea. The fish finally spat him onto the shore, only a day's walk from Nineveh.

Again, God instructed Jonah to go to Nineveh, taking the message that if the people did not change their ways, their city would fall in 40 days. To Jonah's astonishment and dismay, the Ninevites believed the message and repented. Even the king removed his robe, put on sackcloth, and covered himself with ashes as a symbol of repentance.

Jonah was furious when God spared the Ninevites. The Book of Jonah records Jonah's angry conviction that the Ninevites deserved God's punishment, and instead God forgave them. Jonah said he would rather die than see his enemies receive mercy instead of punishment. In disgust, he walked outside the city gates, built a small shelter for himself, and waited for God to punish the Ninevites.

While waiting, Jonah learned a sobering lesson at God's hands. God made a broad-leafed plant grow to provide shade for Jonah, but then God sent a worm to kill the plant and remove the shade. As the hot wind and sun beat down on Jonah's head, Jonah once again said he would rather die than live. Then God spelled out his lesson in detail, saying, "You are concerned about the bush, for which you did not labor...should I not be concerned about Nineveh, that great city, in which there are more than a hundred and twenty thousand persons?" (Jonah 4:9–11).

For further study, see Jonah; Nahum 1:1; 3:1; Zephaniah 2:13–15; Matthew 12:39–41; 16:4; Luke 11:29–32.

❖

JONATHAN (JAHN uh thuhn) *the Lord has given;* 11 century B.C.; 1 Samuel 13:2

As King Saul's son and heir, Jonathan may have expected to reign himself one day, but instead he stepped aside for David, a friend who was closer than a brother. The relationship between Jonathan and David is one of the Bible's great models of friendship and loyalty.

Jonathan's friendship with David began when King Saul honored the young shepherd for killing the Philistine champion, Goliath. Jonathan made a symbolic gesture of friendship, giving David his tunic and weapons as a pledge. Despite his father's growing animosity toward David, Jonathan remained a true friend, risking his father's anger and his own life to defend David.

Later, Saul, Jonathan, and two of his brothers died in a battle with the Philistines, and David grieved for the whole family. The final piece of Jonathan's story occurred when David found Jonathan's only surviving relative, a lame son named Mephibosheth, and provided for him out of his love for Jonathan.

For further study, see 1 Samuel 13–14; 18–20; 2 Samuel 1; 4:4; 9:1–13.

❖

JOSEPH (JOH suhf; son of Jacob)
may God add; 18 century B.C.;
Genesis 30:24

When Jacob was young, his mother favored him, while his father favored his twin, Esau. This rivalry hurt both brothers and nearly destroyed their family. By practicing the same kind of favoritism toward his own 12 sons, Jacob provoked conflict among the brothers and initiated a story that ultimately teaches forgiveness, loyalty, and God's foresight.

Jacob had a richly ornamented coat made for Joseph—a show of preference for his eleventh son that made the other brothers angry and jealous. These feelings were aggravated when Joseph began having dreams that showed that he would one day lead the family. When Joseph reported his dreams to the family, the older brothers were outraged, and even his father was disturbed.

Joseph's brothers soon had an opportunity to vent their anger when their father sent Joseph to meet them in the hills. They saw him from a distance, and decided to kill him, throw his body into a pit, and claim that wild animals had attacked the boy.

Reuben, the eldest, was appalled at the idea. Thinking quickly, he suggested they throw Joseph into a pit and leave him for dead, after which Reuben planned to secretly rescue him. The brothers accepted this proposal. When Joseph arrived, they seized him, stripped the coat from his body, and threw him into a pit. Traders bound for Egypt later passed by, and their presence sparked a cruel idea: Why not sell their brother and make a profit? Since Reuben was elsewhere, Joseph had no advocate; they sold their 17-year-old brother into slavery for 20 pieces of silver.

Joseph was later sold to Potiphar, captain of Pharaoh's guard. In time, Potiphar recognized his young servant's skill and trustworthiness and made Joseph his steward. Where Potiphar saw skill, his wife saw a handsome face. She repeatedly attempted to seduce Joseph, once grabbing his garment as he pulled away from her. Hurt by his rejections, she accused him of attempted rape and used his garment as evidence. No slave could disprove such an accusation, and Joseph was imprisoned.

During this time, Pharaoh's personal cupbearer and baker were imprisoned too. Both men had peculiar dreams, and when they complained to Joseph that no interpretation was possible, he remarked that true interpretations came from God and offered to consult the God of Israel on their behalf. After listening to their dreams, Joseph told the cupbearer that Pharaoh would free him in three days and told the baker that Pharaoh would execute him in three days. In keeping with Joseph's interpretations, the baker was executed and the cupbearer returned to his duties at court, but he forgot about Joseph altogether.

Two years later, Pharaoh also had a dream, which so disturbed him that he sent for magicians and wise men to ask for an interpretation. When no one could interpret Pharaoh's dream, the cupbearer's memory and conscience struck him simultaneously. He told Pharaoh about the incident in prison and Joseph's remarkable interpretation of the dreams, so Pharaoh sent for Joseph at once.

Joseph heard Pharaoh's dream and told Pharaoh that seven good years would be followed by seven years of terrible famine. He then outlined a plan by which the Egyptians could be saved from starvation. The plan so pleased Pharaoh that he appointed Joseph as overseer of the kingdom with authority to organize grain storage for the next seven years.

When the famine came, it was so great that even in Canaan, Jacob and his sons ran out of food. This forced Jacob to send his sons to Egypt, where they begged Joseph for food—though they were unaware of his true identity. After a series of events in which Joseph tested his brothers, Joseph revealed himself, forgave his brothers, and was reunited with his father and brother. At his death, Joseph asked to be buried in Canaan, a request that was honored generations later when Moses took Joseph's remains back to Canaan during the Exodus.

> *Joseph began having dreams that showed that he would one day lead the family.*

For further study, see Genesis 30:22; 35:16–26; 37; 39–50; Exodus 1:1–8; 13:19; Joshua 24:32.

❖

JOSEPH (father of Jesus); A.D. 1 century; Matthew 1:16

According to the Gospel of Matthew, Joseph was a descendant of David and a man of integrity, honor, and loyalty, but he was not the biological father of Jesus. When Joseph learned that his betrothed Mary was carrying someone else's child, he chose to end their engagement by quietly divorcing her. A "quiet divorce" (one involving just two other witnesses) would have saved Mary from the public disgrace of full court action against her. Joseph went through with the marriage, however, after an angel appeared to him in a dream, saying that the child was "of the Holy Spirit" (Matthew 1:20).

Joseph protected Jesus, fleeing with his family to Egypt to escape the wrath and murderous intent of King Herod the Great. He also took Jesus to Jerusalem for the rite of purification or circumcision at the prescribed time. After returning with his family to Nazareth of Galilee, Joseph trained his son in the family business of carpentry.

According to Matthew 13:55, Joseph was the father of several children by Mary—four sons and several daughters. Although Mary and Jesus' brothers are mentioned throughout the Gospels, Joseph is conspicuously absent from all but the earliest years of Jesus' life.

For further study, see Matthew 1:16—2:23; 12:46; 13:55–57; Mark 3:31; 6:3; Luke 1:26–38; 2:1–52; 4:22; John 2:12; 6:42; 7:3, 27–28; 19:26–27; 1 Corinthians 9:5; Galatians 1:19.

❖

JOSEPH OF ARIMATHEA; A.D. 1 century; Matthew 27:57

Joseph of Arimathea, a wealthy and respected member of the Sanhedrin (the high Jewish council) did not take part in its plot of to put Jesus to death. In fact, Joseph himself was a disciple of Jesus, something he kept secret because of his fear of the other Pharisees. After the crucifixion of Jesus, Joseph secured permission from Pilate to remove the body of Jesus from the cross. He then provided fine linen for the burial, laid the body in his own unused rock tomb, and rolled a huge stone to the door of the tomb.

For further study, see Matthew 27:57–59; Mark 15:43–46; Luke 23:50–53; John 19:38.

❖

JOSHUA (JAHSH oo uh) *the Lord is salvation;* 15 century B.C.; Exodus 17:9

Under Moses' leadership, the ancient Israelites were freed from slavery and oppression in Egypt. As they traveled through the wilderness to return to their ancient homeland, Moses chose and trained leaders to assist him, and among the most gifted of these leaders was Joshua.

Soon after the Israelites' successful escape from Pharaoh, they were forced to fight for their lives against the Amalekites at Rephidim. Joshua led the Hebrew defense in a battle now famous in Israel's history because his troops were victorious only as long as Moses stood on the hillside with his staff raised. If Moses' arm dropped, the Amalekites gained advantage. Evidently, Joshua's success in battle earned him his new name.

Joshua appeared at crucial points in the establishment of Israel as a spiritual and political nation. When Moses brought the people north from Mt. Sinai to the oasis of Kadesh-barnea, they stood at the doorway to Canaan, the land God had promised to give them as a home. Joshua was chosen to represent his tribe, Ephraim, on the team sent to survey the land. Twelve Hebrew men traveled some 40 days through Canaan to spy out the quality of the land and assess military strength. They discovered rich farm and grazing lands and beautiful countryside. However, they also found fortified cities and numerous armies, including the tall, powerful-looking Anakite tribesmen. The spies were frightened. Upon their return, they gave exaggerated reports that the country was populated by giants who could not possibly be defeated. Only Joshua and Caleb of Judah disagreed, as they were confident of Israel's military strength and God's support. Upon hearing reports about giants, the people wailed like mourners. When they began to talk about going back to Egypt, Joshua and Caleb tore their clothes in grief and begged the people to trust God's protection. The angry crowd nearly stoned them.

> *Moses chose and trained leaders to assist him, and among the most gifted of these leaders was Joshua.*

Divine punishment for this lack of faith was quick to come and long in duration. Moses delivered the judgment: Even though the Israelites had been miraculously rescued from Egypt, they still did not believe. God's patience was ended; he would not permit any of the adults, except the families of Moses, Joshua, and Caleb, to enter Canaan. Ten of the spies died of plague, and the Israelites lived as nomads for 40 years in the deserts near Kadesh-barnea.

Toward the end of this period, Moses officially recognized Joshua as Israel's new leader. The priest Eleazar blessed Joshua to confirm him as leader, judge, and preserver of the Law. The task of leading the Israelites into the Promised Land was a risky, bold endeavor. All of Joshua's military skill and faith in God were fully tested as his band of desert-dwelling nomads invaded fortified cities and challenged standing armies.

Before his death, Joshua gathered his people for a final word. He reaffirmed that God would give them all the land between the River Jordan and the western coast, warned them about idol worship and foreign gods, and challenged them in the strongest terms that they had to choose between the God of Israel and the Egyptian idols their ancestors worshipped. Joshua's personal statement of faith has been repeated in words of commitment over the centuries. He said, "...choose this day whom you will serve...but as for me and my household, we will serve the Lord" (Joshua 24:15).

For further study, see Exodus 14; 17:8–16; 24:12–18; 32:1; 33:11; Numbers 13–14; 26:65; 27:12–23; Deuteronomy 1:19–40; 3:21–29; 31–34; Joshua.

❖

JOSIAH (joh SIGH uh) *the Lord supports* or *fire of the Lord;* ruled 640–609 B.C.; 1 Kings 13:2

After the reign of Solomon, son of the legendary King David, Israel split into separate nations, Israel and Judah. During this era of political and ethnic division, Josiah became Judah's sixteenth ruler. Although Josiah's grandfather had burned one of his own children as an offering to the pagan god Baal, and his father worshipped idols all his life, Josiah worshipped Israel's God.

During the eighteenth year of Josiah's reign, renovation work was being done in the temple. At the king's order, the high priest Hilkiah reviewed the temple treasury in preparation for this significant expense. During the review, a Book of the Law was found (perhaps segments or an ancient copy of the Book of Deuteronomy).

The book was read to King Josiah, who listened intently to its descriptions of God's spiritual and moral standards. Josiah saw immediately how far the Hebrew people had strayed from God's ways and was horrified. He tore his clothes in a sign of grief and told the high priest to pray for the nation, because their disobedience surely deserved God's anger. Josiah did not know what to do. The priests consulted a respected prophet, Huldah, who confirmed Josiah's trepidation; she said God would destroy Judah, although not during his lifetime.

Josiah ordered the entire nation to the temple and required everyone, from the highest priest to the simplest laborer, to listen to God's commandments. To underscore their importance, Josiah read the words himself and made a public promise to keep God's decrees. This public reading of the Law began an era

of radical reform. Josiah started in the temple, taking all vessels or items connected with the worship of Baal, Asherah, or other idols to be burned. He deposed Hebrew priests who made offerings to Baal, tore down buildings that housed temple prostitutes, and ground idols to dust. He attempted to stop the child sacrifice practiced by worshippers of the Ammonite god Milcom by defiling the entry to the valley of Hinnom, where the vile practice occurred.

Josiah also commanded a celebration of Passover in Jerusalem in the reconsecrated temple. This celebration revived not only the religious tradition of recalling God's rescue of the Hebrew people from slavery in Egypt, but also their ancient identity as a nation set apart by God.

For further study, see 1 Kings 13:1–4; 2 Kings 21:24; 22–23; 2 Chronicles 34–36; Jeremiah 1:1–3; Zephaniah 1:1–6.

❖

JUDAH (JOO duh) *praised;*
18 century B.C.; Genesis 29:35

Judah is among the best-known sons of Jacob because his offspring became the tribe of Judah from which came King David and the Messiah Jesus.

Judah grew up in a divided, jealous household. His father, Jacob, had married his two cousins Rachel and Leah, but Jacob loved only Rachel and favored her two sons over his other sons. Judah and most of his brothers so hated Joseph, because he was favored by their father, that they considered killing him. Later, at Judah's suggestion, they sold the boy to traveling Midianite slave traders. Joseph ended up in Egypt, where he prospered. Years later, Joseph saved his father, his brothers, and their extended families from starvation.

Earlier, Judah had married a Canaanite woman and had fathered three sons—Er, Onan, and Shelah. Er married Tamar but died soon after, leaving her widowed and childless. In that culture, a brother-in-law was required to take a childless widow as his own wife and father her children, who would be recognized as his brother's children. Since Onan did not want to father and raise children only to have them recognized as his brother's offspring, Onan intentionally avoided impregnating Tamar. This so displeased the Lord that Onan died also. Judah sent Tamar to her father's home to live as a widow until his youngest son, Shelah, became an adult. Tamar remained there until it became obvious that Judah would never keep his promise because he feared that Shelah, too, would die.

Tamar was desperate; not only would she be left without support when her father died, but also her childlessness was considered shameful. Since Judah

> *Jacob promised that Judah would rule, and the staff of leadership would not be taken from him or his descendants.*

would not fulfill his obligations, Tamar dressed as a prostitute and waited by the side of the road for Judah. When he offered a goat in payment for her services, she demanded his staff, cord, and signet ring to hold until she received payment. Judah had his pleasure, but later, a servant sent to deliver the goat and collect the items left in pledge returned with this surprising news: Not only had the woman disappeared, but no prostitute even lived in the area. When Tamar became pregnant, Judah accused her of prostitution and was prepared to kill her. However, when she produced the staff, cord, and signet ring, Judah acknowledged his sin against her and accepted her twin sons as his own.

While the clan was in Egypt, Jacob grew frail and ill. As his father before him had done, Jacob blessed his sons before he died. In that day, a father's blessing was more than good wishes; it held spiritual power and, in Jacob's case, was prophetic as well. Jacob said his other sons would bow down to Judah. He called Judah a lion, indicating fearsome strength in battle. Finally, Jacob promised that Judah would rule, and the staff of leadership would not be taken from him or his descendants.

Throughout the history of Israel, the tribe of Judah led and was more powerful than the other Jewish tribes. After the reign of Solomon, the nation split into separate kingdoms, northern Israel and southern Judah, and Judah's kingdom included the holy city of Jerusalem.

For further study, see Genesis 37–38; 42:18–34; 46:12; 49:1, 8–12; Numbers 1:26–27; Joshua 15:1–12; Matthew 1:1–3.

❖

JUDAS ISCARIOT (JOO duhs is KAYR ee uht); A.D. 1 century; Matthew 10:4

Few names in history carry the stigma borne by the name Judas Iscariot. Judas was one of the 12 disciples, although the New Testament records little except that he was not Galilean and that Jesus entrusted him with the group's money. In his Gospel, John calls Judas a thief for stealing coins from their money bag. Along with Mark, John also records that Judas criticized Mary of Bethany for anointing Jesus' feet with costly ointment. These references highlight the greed that marked his character.

On Passover night, before his death, Jesus washed all the disciples' feet—including Judas's—yet predicted one would betray him. John's Gospel clearly indicates Jesus knew the betrayer was Judas. Late that night, Judas contacted the chief priests and led the temple guards to the garden of Gethsemane. There, in an act that deeply saddened

Jesus, Judas identified his Master by a kiss of greeting.

Judas received 30 pieces of silver for his treachery, but after Jesus' arrest he returned the money, saying, "I have sinned by betraying innocent blood" (Matthew 27:4). Judas then hung himself. The priests used the tainted silver to buy a pauper's cemetery, appropriately called the "Field of Blood."

For further study, see Matthew 26:14–25; 26:47—27:10; Mark 14:10–21, 43–53; Luke 22:3–23, 47–53; John 12:1–8; 18:2–12.

❖

 LABAN (LAY buhn) *white;* **20 century B.C.; Genesis 24:29**

To escape the wrath of his brother Esau whose birthright he had stolen, Jacob sought sanctuary with his mother's brother Laban. Laban was known for shrewd dealings in everything from marriage and dowry arrangements to labor and management negotiations, and he had two daughters to marry off, Leah and Rachel.

Jacob agreed to work seven years for Laban if he could then marry the younger daughter, Rachel. But on the wedding night, Laban substituted Leah for Rachel under the wedding veil, and once Jacob and Leah had slept together, the marriage was consummated. When Jacob awoke next to the wrong woman, he realized too late that Laban had tricked him. When Jacob confronted Laban, he said he had carried out the deception only because it was necessary to marry off his older daughter before he could let the younger one wed; in truth, he feared he might not be able to find a husband for Leah. Jacob then agreed to take Rachel as his second wife and work seven more years for Laban.

Before he was done scheming, Laban had contracted for Jacob's services indefinitely. Jacob agreed to work in exchange for a share of the family sheep flocks, but Laban repeatedly gave Jacob less than he had earned. Still Jacob managed to accrue sizable wealth from his service for Laban. Eventually, much to Laban's dismay, Jacob was able to return home, taking Leah, Rachel, and their children with him.

For further study, see Genesis 24; 27:41–28:5; 29:1–30; 30:25; 32:5; 46:18.

❖

LAZARUS (LAZ uh ruhs) *God has helped;* A.D. 1 century; John 11:1
Lazarus and his sisters, Martha and Mary, were Jesus' friends. Jesus found comfort and welcome at their home in Bethany. Once, Lazarus became seriously ill, and his sisters sent for Jesus. After waiting for two days, Jesus announced to his disciples that they should go with him to Bethany because Lazarus had died. Jesus said he had purposely delayed so the disciples might see a miracle even greater than healing.

When Jesus arrived, Lazarus had been dead four days. Amidst cries that the decomposing body would smell badly, Jesus ordered that the stone be rolled away from Lazarus's tomb door. Jesus prayed, then shouted, "Lazarus, come out," and Lazarus emerged alive, still wrapped in his burial cloths. When news of this miracle reached Jerusalem, some Jewish leaders feared everyone would follow Jesus, whom they considered a false messiah, so they began making plans to do away with both Jesus and Lazarus.

For further study, see John 11:1—12:11.

❖

LEAH (LEE uh) *wild cow;* 18 century B.C.; Genesis 29:16
Leah became Jacob's first wife through deception. Jacob had arranged to marry Leah's sister Rachel, but on the day of the wedding, Rachel's father sent Leah in her place, disguised behind a veil. Jacob did not discover Leah's true identity until after the marriage had been consummated and so had no recourse but to accept her as his first wife. He later took Rachel as his second wife and greatly favored her over Leah.

Through her sorrow, Leah learned to place her trust and affection in God, who blessed her with six sons and one daughter. With each child, her faith deepened. The Lord honored her by making her an ancestor of King David and the promised Messiah Jesus.

For further study, see Genesis 27:41—28:5; 29:1—30:24; 49:31; Matthew 1:2–3.

❖

LEVI (LEE vye) *joined;* 20 century B.C.; Genesis 29:34

Levi was the third son of Jacob by his wife Leah. The priestly tribe of Israel bears his name. The descendants of his three sons later became the ancestral heads of the three main divisions of the priesthood—the Gershonites, the Kohathites, and the Merarites.

Levi and his brother Simeon are noted for their violent revenge of the rape of their sister Dinah; they massacred an entire town rather than punishing the one man who had committed the crime. Living up to this reputation for violence, the sons of Levi killed 3,000 Hebrew rebels who defied Moses during the Exodus in the wilderness.

The tribe of Levi received no inheritance in the Promised Land in part to free them to fulfill their priestly duties. And one of Levi's descendants was the great lawgiver, Moses.

For further study, see Genesis 29:34; 34:25–31; 35:23; 46:11; 49:5–7; Exodus 1:2; 6:16; 32:25–29; Numbers 3–4; 16:1; 18:20–24; 26:59; Joshua 21; 1 Chronicles 2:1; 6:1–47; Ezra 8:18.

❖

LOT (LAHT) *concealed* or *covering;* 22 century B.C.; Genesis 11:27

Born at Ur of the Chaldees (in southern Iraq), Lot traveled with his father Haran and uncle Abraham, who was responding to God's call and promise of land and descendants. However, Lot separated himself from that godly influence and settled in the well-watered, well-populated Jordan area among "cities of the plain" (at the southern end of the Dead Sea). There he pursued the comforts and customs of the wicked city of Sodom. Against God's will, Lot not only moved his tent near Sodom but soon was "sitting in the gateway" as an elder of the sinful city.

Two angels, however, warned Lot of God's plan to destroy Sodom and told him he and his family must flee or be destroyed as well. For associating with such sinners, Lot paid dearly with the loss of his goods and his wife, who was turned into a "pillar of salt" for disobeying the angels' instructions.

Eventually, Lot and his descendants settled in the mountainous land of Moab. With his own two daughters, Lot conceived two sons—Moab and Ben-ammi, ancestors of the Moabites and Ammonites, respectively.

For further study, see Genesis 11:27–31; 12:4–5; 13:1—14:16; 19:1–36; Deuteronomy 2:9–19; Luke 17:28–29; 2 Peter 2:7.

❖

LUKE (LEWK) *light* or *bright;* A.D. 1 century; Colossians 4:14

Paul knew him best as a traveling companion, a "fellow worker," "fellow prisoner," and as "the beloved physician." Luke accompanied Paul as he traveled from Troas to Philippi and later from Philippi to Jerusalem. He also accompanied Paul during his final voyage to Rome.

Readers of the Bible know Luke best as the author of the Gospel bearing his name, as well as the Acts of the Apostles. Luke's writings comprise a quarter of the New Testament. His two volumes show careful attention to geographic, nautical, and medical terminology, and give specific information about the political and historical backdrop of the time.

The only non-Jewish author of a New Testament book, Luke spoke for the poor and oppressed of society; his Gospel included people normally rendered unacceptable by the religious or social elite of the time. Luke presents Jesus as the universal Savior, both in terms of history (tracing Jesus' genealogy back to Adam and Eve) and in terms of ethnic inclusivity. Luke's Gospel focuses on Gentiles, Romans, Samaritans, women, lepers, children, tax collectors, and prostitutes—any and all who fell outside the purview of ancient Judaism.

For further study, see Luke; Acts; Colossians 4:10–17; 2 Timothy 4:11; Philemon 1:24.

> *The only non-Jewish author of a New Testament book, Luke spoke for the poor and oppressed of society.*

❖

LYDIA (LID ee uh) *meaning unknown;* A.D. 1 century; Acts 16:14

Born in Thyatira of the Lydia region (western Turkey), Lydia later settled in Philippi in Macedonia (modern Greece). There she could market her expensive purple cloth among the social elite, military retirees, and ruling families. When she heard the apostle Paul speak in the business district at Philippi, she reaffirmed the decision she had made earlier to convert to Judaism and worship God alone; she then became Europe's first convert to Christianity and a fine example of a successful Christian woman in the marketplace. She converted her whole household to Christianity and hosted the first European house church.

For further study, see Acts 16:11–15, 40.

❖

MARK (MAHRK)
large hammer; A.D.
1 century; Acts 12:12

Mark had a unique vantage point on the Gospel. The home of Mary, Mark's mother, was probably the secret meeting place not only for the Last Supper and other meetings Jesus had with his disciples but also for the early Christian gatherings recorded in the Acts of the Apostles.

The young Mark (also called John Mark) became a companion of two great missionaries—his cousin Barnabas and the apostle Paul. Mark traveled with them on their first journey from Antioch to Cyprus and Perga in Pamphylia. Without explanation, Mark decided to leave and return home. When planning a second journey with Paul, Barnabas wanted to invite Mark again. Paul steadfastly refused to take someone he considered a deserter. This resulted in a parting of ways between Paul and Barnabas. Barnabas took Mark with him to his native Cyprus, while Paul chose another companion— Silas—to travel with him throughout Syria and Cilicia.

Mark and Paul were evidently reconciled some ten years later, since Paul commended Mark to the church at Colossae, calling him his "fellow worker" and referring to him as "useful in my ministry." Peter referred to "my son Mark" in one of his letters. If Mark was a spiritual son to Peter, then he would have had anecdotes and actual quotes from Peter's life and preaching. After Peter and Paul both suffered a martyr's death, Mark could then have borrowed from Peter's notes in penning his version of the life and ministry of Jesus, which was probably the first Gospel to be circulated.

For further study, see Mark; Acts 12:25; 15:37–39; Colossians 4:10; 2 Timothy 4:11; 1 Peter 5:13.

❖

MARTHA (MAHR thuh) *lady;* A.D. 1 century; Luke 10:38

Martha lived with her brother Lazarus and her sister Mary. They were all close friends of Jesus and often opened up their home to him as he traveled through Bethany. Once, while Mary preferred sitting at Jesus' feet listening to what he said, Martha complained that Mary was not helping her with chores. Jesus gently rebuked Martha because Mary had chosen a better pursuit.

When Lazarus became very ill, the sisters sent for Jesus to come, but he did not arrive until after their brother had died. Martha and Mary were grieving and wondered why Jesus had not come immediately. Jesus assured Martha that Lazarus would "rise again," and she took this as a reference to the final resurrection on the day of judgment. Jesus then said, "I am the resurrection and the life. Those who believe in me, even though they die, will live....Do you believe this?" (John 11:25–26). In one of the most direct and overt professions of faith in the Gospel, Martha proclaimed that Jesus was the Messiah and the Son of God.

For further study, see Luke 10:38–42; John 11:1—12:11.

❖

MARY (MAIR ee) *bitterness;* 1st century B.C.; Matthew 1:18

Mary is introduced in Scripture as a young virgin engaged to Joseph, a descendant of Abraham and David. According to Jewish custom, an engagement was linked to marriage in such a way that the fiancée was called wife. Any sexual relationship during this period was considered adultery. According to Jewish Law, if the wife was proved to be unfaithful, she would be stoned to death.

During her engagement, Mary was visited at her home in Nazareth by the angel Gabriel, who said to her, "Greetings, favored one! The Lord is with you" (Luke 1:28). He then announced that she would become pregnant and have a child who would be called the Son of the Most High and who would inherit the throne of King David and reign forever. Mary answered, "How can this be, since I am a virgin?" (Luke 1:34). She

did not doubt what Gabriel said but was confused about how it could happen. The angel explained that she would become pregnant through the power of the Holy Spirit, and she accepted this assignment for her life in spite of the shame and danger she would experience because of her pregnancy.

Mary received other good news from the angel Gabriel—her older relative Elizabeth had conceived a son six months earlier and was going to have a baby after a long life of childlessness. In Mary's joy, she traveled to the city of Judah in the hill country to visit Elizabeth and her husband Zechariah. When she arrived at their house and greeted them, the baby in Elizabeth's womb (John the Baptist) leaped for joy to hear the voice of the mother of Jesus. Elizabeth exuberantly expressed in a loud voice how blessed she was to be in the presence of Mary and the child she would bear.

> *Mary's song... shows that she was a humble, God-fearing woman.*

Following this demonstration of delight, Mary broke out in a song of praise and adoration to God for what he had done. Mary's song, known historically as the "Magnificat," reflects some of the Old Testament psalms, as well as Hannah's song of praise in First Samuel after her son Samuel was born. This inspiring song demonstrates that Mary was well educated in the Old Testament and shows that she was a humble, God-fearing woman.

Mary returned to Nazareth, where her fiancé Joseph was ready to divorce her quietly rather than expose her to the public shame and punishment imposed on an adulteress in Jewish culture. But Joseph was visited in a dream by an angel who assured him that the child Mary carried was conceived by the Holy Spirit and would save his people from their sins. Joseph took Mary home as his wife.

When Mary was in her last month of pregnancy, Caesar Augustus ordered a census to be taken of the entire Roman world. Mary and Joseph had to register in Bethlehem, the town of David, because Joseph belonged to the house of David. Because of the large influx of people to Bethlehem for the census, Mary and Joseph had no place to stay when she went into labor. The child was born humbly in a place where animals were kept and fed. Mary even graciously accepted guests to this manger-crib when the unexpected shepherds arrived. She later entertained the kings from the East who came to worship Jesus. Mary kept these events in her heart.

Later, an angel told Joseph to flee with his family to Egypt to escape King Herod's attempt to kill Jesus. So Mary and her family were again traveling under adverse conditions, this time leaving in the middle of the night in secrecy. Mary, Joseph, and Jesus stayed in Egypt until Herod died and all danger was past. They returned to Nazareth and lived together as a family while Jesus grew to manhood.

Later, Mary was present at Jesus' first miracle when he changed the water to wine at a wedding in Cana. In fact, she prompted the miracle by telling Jesus that the supply of wine was exhausted and then instructing the servants to obey Jesus' commands. Mary was also present when Jesus was crucified on the cross. She saw the son she bore suffer an indescribably cruel death, but in Jesus' agony, he still looked down at the foot of the cross, saw his mother, and told John, the beloved disciple, to care for her for the rest of her life.

For further study, see Matthew 1:16–25; 13:54–57; Luke 1–2; John 2:1–5; 19:25–27; Acts 1:14; Galatians 4:4.

❖

MARY MAGDALENE; A.D. 1 century; Matthew 27:56

As Jesus and his disciples traveled from town to town, a group of exceptional women followed and financially supported them wherever they went. Mary Magdalene was among these women. Indebted to Jesus, who had liberated her from demon possession, Mary followed him and gave money to his ministry.

Unswerving in her devotion, Mary was at the cross, where she observed

Jesus endure this cruel method of Roman execution. Watching opposite the tomb where Jesus' body was taken, she also witnessed his burial by Joseph of Arimathea. She saw the Romans roll an enormous stone in front of the tomb, closing off and sealing Jesus' burial place. After leaving the tomb, she maintained a vigil through the sabbath until the dawn of the next day and then returned to the tomb with anointing spices.

Atop the stone that had been rolled away from the entrance of the tomb sat a luminous angel—a truly frightening sight for the Roman guards and for Mary. John's Gospel says Mary saw two other angels inside the tomb who asked her why she was crying. Mary then turned to see a man she thought was the gardener. She asked him to tell her where he might have carried Jesus' body. But when the man spoke her name, Mary recognized his voice—it was Jesus. She then called him *Rabboni,* meaning My Teacher. After Jesus told her to go tell the disciples what she had heard, Mary immediately ran to tell them the news of his resurrection and the things Jesus had told her.

For further study, see Matthew 27:56–61; 28:1; Mark 15:40–47; 16:1–9; Luke 8:2; 24:10; John 19:25; 20:1–18.

❖

MATTHEW (MATH yoo) *gift of the Lord;* A.D. 1 century; Matthew 9:9

Unlike the rugged fishermen that Jesus had already called as disciples, Matthew (or Levi) worked as a Roman government employee—a detested tax collector, or publican. Jews who collected taxes for Rome were despised as traitors to their own people. Many also collected more taxes than Rome demanded, lining their pockets at the expense of their own people. Due to their bad reputation and bad business practices, publicans were generally referred to as sinners.

Jesus first approached Matthew as he sat at his collection booth, simply saying "Follow me." Responding to this call, Matthew left his booth and became one of Jesus' followers. That day, he invited Jesus to dinner at his home, which was obviously visible to outsiders, for the Pharisees saw what was going on in Matthew's dining room and asked the disciples why Jesus was eating with tax collectors and sinners. Jesus defended his friendship with Matthew and everyone with whom he was sharing his meal when he said, "For I have come to call not the righteous but sinners" (Matthew 9:13).

Matthew later wrote the Gospel that was specifically written to show his Jewish brethren that Jesus was indeed their long-awaited Messiah, for it is filled with Hebrew prophecies.

For further study, see Matthew; Mark 2:13–17; 3:18; Luke 6:15; Acts 1:13.

❖

MELCHIZEDEK (mel KIZ uh dek) *king of righteousness;* 22 century B.C.; Genesis 14:18

At the time Abraham met Melchizedek, he was king of Salem (short form of Jerusalem) and a priest of the Most High God. This was a most propitious meeting at which this king-priest interceded on Abraham's behalf. Melchizedek offered bread and wine to the war-weary Abraham, as well as a prayer of blessing for him and praise to God for victory over Abraham's enemies. For this service, Abraham gave Melchizedek a tithe of all the bounty won in battle.

The Melchizedek mentioned in the Book of Psalms may be the same Melchizedek mentioned in the Genesis account, or he may be the more symbolic idealized king-priest who would foreshadow Jesus' priestly ministry. According to the writer of Hebrews, the priesthood of Melchizedek was greater than the person of Abraham (whom he blessed and received a tithe from) and greater than the Levitical or Aaronic priesthood (since Levi, being a descendant of Abraham, was subordinate to Abraham; hence also to Melchizedek). The greatness of Melchizedek would be exceeded only by Christ's perfect priesthood.

For further study, see Genesis 14:17–24; Psalm 110:4; Hebrews 5:5–10; 6:19—7:17.

❖

MICHAL (MY kuhl) *who is like God?;* 11 century B.C.; 1 Samuel 18:20

After King Saul gave his daughter Michal to David in marriage, he tried to kill David. Michal, however, courageously protected her husband from her father, even sneaking David out a window and placing an idol with fake hair in bed with her when Saul sent soldiers to kill him. While David was in hiding, Saul gave Michal to Paltiel in marriage. When David became king after Saul's death, he sent for Michal, but their marriage was not the same. Her bitter cynicism surfaced when she ridiculed David for dancing naked and joyfully before the ark when it was returned to Jerusalem. Her rebuke marked the end of their once romantic relationship, and she bore no children as a result.

For further study, see 1 Samuel 14:49; 18:20—19:17; 2 Samuel 6:12–23; 3:12–16.

❖

MIRIAM (MEER ee uhm) *meaning unknown;* 15 century B.C.; Exodus 2:4

Miriam was born at a turbulent time in Jewish history—a time when the Israelites were oppressed slaves in Egypt.

When Miriam was just a young girl of 12, the king of Egypt ordered

Shiphrah and Puah, two Hebrew midwives, to slaughter all Jewish baby boys as soon as they were born in order to control the Hebrew population. After Miriam's mother, Jochebed, gave birth to Moses, Jochebed built a basket out of papyrus, water proofed it with tar, placed Moses in it, and hid the basket among the reeds. Miriam helped by keeping a vigil, faithfully watching the little makeshift lifeboat from a discreet distance to see where it landed down river. Pharaoh's daughter discovered the basket. Though she recognized the baby as a Hebrew, she wanted to keep the child. Miriam offered to fetch a Hebrew woman to nurse the baby. Pharaoh's daughter jumped at the chance to hire Jochebed as a nursemaid for the baby.

During the Exodus of the Israelites from Egypt and their subsequent 40 years in the desert, Miriam shared leadership with her brothers Moses and Aaron. After the miracle of the Red Sea (when God parted the waters, allowing the Israelites to cross to safety on dry land), Miriam expressed her elation with song and dance. With tambourine in hand, she began to play and sing in praise and thanksgiving to God.

However, Miriam did not always sing praises to God for what he did, and she did not always support her brother

> *After the miracle of the Red Sea ... Miriam expressed her elation with song and dance.*

Moses. She and Aaron both spoke against Moses when he married a Cushite (Ethiopian) woman, but their irritation with Moses went beyond his choice of a wife. Miriam and Aaron rebelled against his leadership because they were jealous and envious of his position of authority over Israel. They decided to express their resentment publicly: "Has the Lord spoken only through Moses? Has he not spoken through us also?" (Numbers 12:2).

No mention is made of how Moses reacted to his siblings' accusations, but God responded immediately and decisively. He called all three to the Tent of Meeting, where he appeared to them in a cloud. He spoke directly to Miriam and Aaron, rebuking them for talking behind Moses' back and rebelling against his authority. Miriam was then left standing with leprosy that covered her entire body. In his anguish, Aaron begged Moses to forgive them of their sin. So Moses cried out to God to heal Miriam. God did heal her, but only after she was led away from the people and quarantined outside the camp for seven days. Miriam is not mentioned again until her death and burial at Kadesh in the Wilderness of Zin.

For further study, see Exodus 15:20–21; Numbers 12:1–15; 20:1;

26:59; Deuteronomy 24:9; 1 Chronicles 6:3; Micah 6:4.

❖

MORDECAI (MOHR duh kye)
consecrated to Marduk [a Sumerian god]; 5 century B.C.; Esther 2:5

Mordecai was the adoptive father of his orphaned cousin Esther. He raised Esther to respect her Jewish roots. Later, after she was selected to marry King Ahasuerus and become the Queen of Persia, she won the king's favor for her fellow Jews in exile and, with the help of Mordecai, reversed a death sentence against her people.

Mordecai came into conflict with the Persian prime minister Haman when he refused to bow down before Haman because he felt that such an act would be idolatrous. The vain Haman was outraged and plotted revenge against not just Mordecai but his people as well by ordering all Jews in Persia to be killed. Fortunately, Mordecai had gained the king's favor by earlier thwarting a plot against the king's life. Ironically, the king ordered Haman to oversee a procession in honor of his enemy Mordecai, which only served to fuel Haman's rage. In the end, Mordecai and Esther exposed Haman's murderous plot against the Jews to the king, who then ordered Haman to be hung on the gallows. Further, Mordecai was given Haman's position as prime minister. The Feast of Purim, which is celebrated to this day by Jews grateful for their historic deliverance by Mordecai and Esther, came to be called Mordecai's Day by some Jews.

For further study, see Esther 2–10.

❖

MOSES (MO zuhs) *draw out;*
15 century B.C.; Exodus 2:2

For centuries the Israelites had been slaves in Egypt. Nevertheless, the Hebrew population continued to grow. Because Pharaoh was afraid of their large numbers, he ordered Hebrew midwives to kill all newborn Hebrew boys. When they refused to obey, the king ordered his own people to drown the babies in the Nile River. It was in this setting that Jochebed and Amram of the tribe of Levi gave birth to a son. She hid her son for three months, but when he grew more active, she put him in a basket made of papyrus and waterproofed with tar. Ironically, she stationed the basket among the reeds of the Nile, the death site for Hebrew babies. Pharaoh's daughter found the baby, named him Moses, and adopted him as her own.

Forty years after his birth, Moses visited the Hebrews as they toiled under the hands of their Egyptian slavemasters. After witnessing an Egyptian beating one of the Hebrews, Moses murdered the Egyptian. Fearing he would be executed for the crime, Moses fled to Midian. There he married and began a life as a shepherd.

One day, as Moses led his flock by Mt. Horeb, an angel of God appeared to him in the fire of a burning bush. As Moses came near the bush, God spoke directly to him, warning him not to come any closer and to take off his sandals, for he was standing on holy ground.

In their despair, the Israelites had cried out to God to be released from slavery. God heard their cries and decided to free them through Moses. But Moses was not sure he was the man to do the job. He questioned God time and time again, which prompted God to perform miracles so Moses would believe. Moses saw his staff become a snake and the snake become a staff again. He saw his own hand turn leprous, and he saw it restored. Still, Moses hesitated, saying he was not a good speaker, so God told him that his older brother, Aaron, would speak for him.

Despite Moses' self-doubt, he returned to Egypt and told Pharaoh to let his people go. At first, Pharaoh refused, but after ten plagues that devastated Egypt, he reluctantly relented. These plagues were an incredible display of God's power over the deadly forces of nature. They amazed not only the Israelites' enemies inside and outside of Egypt but also the Hebrew people themselves.

> *Moses raised his staff over the waters, and the Lord parted them to create a path of escape.*

Moses led the Israelites out of Egypt. Shortly after their departure, Pharaoh sought revenge and pursued them with his army. He caught up with them at the mighty Red Sea. There seemed to be no way for the Hebrews to cross the water. Apparently trapped and sure to be captured, the scared Israelites blamed Moses for leading them to destruction. Responding to God's directive, Moses raised his staff over the waters, and God parted them to create a path of escape. When the Egyptian soldiers attempted to pursue the Israelites, the waters rushed together and drowned them.

Later, God gave Moses the Law on Mt. Sinai, where Moses spent 40 days and nights alone with God. After Moses came down from the mountain, he discovered a golden calf that the people had built and worshipped in their impatience for his return. Moses broke the two tablets of God's Law and then fell prostrate and fasted for 40 days and nights, begging God not to completely destroy the people. Although God killed many of the idolaters, he spared most of the Hebrew people and later gave Moses an identical set of stone tablets.

As Moses led a grumbling, complaining nation across the desert to Canaan, God provided water, manna, and quail for them. After many years of wandering, Moses effectively led the rebellious Israelites to the edge of the Promised Land, but on one occasion, the people complained that there was no water. God provided for them again by telling Moses to speak to a rock so that it would produce water. Instead of speaking to the rock, Moses twice struck it with his rod. His years of faithfulness and obedience were tainted by this single disobedient act, and he was not allowed to enter the Promised Land.

Moses died in the desert of Moab after spending another period of private time with God, who showed him a panoramic view of the Promised Land from the top of Mt. Nebo. An epitaph at the end of Deuteronomy gives tribute to Moses, who performed miracles and showed God's mighty power in memorable and amazing ways.

For further study, see Exodus 2–40; Numbers and Deuteronomy.

❖

 NAOMI (nay OH mee) *pleasantness* or *my joy;* 12 century B.C.; Ruth 1:2

In the days when judges guided Israel, a famine forced many people to leave the country. Naomi, her husband Elimelech, and their two sons Mahlon and Chilion

went to Moab, where food was more plentiful. While there, Elimelech died, leaving Naomi a widow and a single parent in a foreign country.

As many in her situation would do, Naomi cherished her sons as they grew. Her joy was great when they married fine Moabite women named Orpah and Ruth. But after ten years in Moab, both of her sons died, and Naomi grieved again.

Naomi's bitterness turned to joy.

When Naomi heard that food was plentiful in Israel once more, she prepared to return to Bethlehem with her daughters-in-law. However, as she thought more about taking these two women out of their own land, she changed her plans and told them to go back to their own mothers. Orpah and Ruth both wept openly and confirmed their decision to go with Naomi, but Naomi insisted they return to their homes. In the end, Orpah finally said good-bye to Naomi, but Ruth clung to her and expressed her devotion and commitment to her dead husband's mother.

Naomi and Ruth arrived in Bethlehem, where Naomi changed her name to Mara, which means bitter, "for the Almighty has dealt bitterly with me." It was Naomi who convinced Ruth to work for a respectable relative named Boaz. He later bought from Naomi the land that had belonged to Elimelech and his two sons and took Ruth as his wife. Naomi's bitterness turned to joy.

For further study, see Ruth.

❖

NATHAN (NAY thuhn) *gift;* 11 century B.C.; 2 Samuel 7:2

Nathan, God's prophet and messenger to King David, reported good news as well as bad to the king. After supporting David's idea to build a temple to replace the portable tentlike tabernacle, Nathan disappointed the enthusiastic king when God revealed that his temple was to be built by David's successor, Solomon.

Later, this prophet confronted King David over his adulterous affair with Bathsheba and the murder of her husband, Uriah. Nathan was cautious in approaching David about the subject. He told a story of a rich man who slaughtered a poor man's beloved pet lamb to serve a meal to a traveler. David condemned himself without realizing it when he told Nathan to make the man pay a fourfold retribution for the lamb and then put the man to death for his crime. Nathan told David that he was the man in his story and that David would endure God's judgment for taking Bathsheba from her husband. As punishment, Nathan informed David that his son by Bathsheba would die.

For further study, see 2 Samuel 7:2–17; 12:1–25; 1 Kings 1:8–45; 4:4–5; 1 Chronicles 17:1–15.

❖

NEHEMIAH (NEE uh MYE uh) *the Lord;* 5 century B.C.; Nehemiah 1:1

Nehemiah is renowned for putting together the many components of a long-term urban renewal strategy to rebuild Jerusalem after its destruction and the people's 70-year captivity in Babylon. Nehemiah's story takes place in Persia (modern Iran), where he worked as a cupbearer in the royal palace. A trusted official, he tasted the food for the Persian king Artaxerxes I. Nehemiah grieved and prayed when he heard that war and pestilence were devastating his beloved Jerusalem. Appealing to his Persian master for help, he received a leave of absence, a letter of credit from the Persian king, and a government grant of timber from Asaph, the national forester. With these resources, Nehemiah began to rebuild Jerusalem.

For his first three days back in Jerusalem, Nehemiah surveyed the community's needs without being intrusive. Townspeople recognized his authority as coming from both God and the king. Indeed, the people responded to his vision with anticipation and solidarity. He organized the people of Judah and centered them on the task of rebuilding the walls of Jerusalem. As the work progressed, their sense of pride, of community, and of heritage began to return.

While the actual rebuilding of the walls took only 52 days, the redevelopment of the systems and values that hold a city together took generations. Nehemiah worked to address the decayed social conditions of his people. He initiated economic reforms to help restore the impoverished region and led a movement to revive the Jews' cultural traditions. With Nehemiah's support, the priest Ezra led his people in worship, in Bible study, and in the renewal of their covenant vows as families and as a community.

For further study, see Nehemiah.

❖

NICODEMUS (NIK uh DEE muhs)
victor over the people; A.D. 1 century; John 3:1

Nicodemus was a Pharisee who held a position on the Sanhedrin, the Jewish high council and ruling body. When Nicodemus came to talk to Jesus in the middle of the night, Jesus told him he had to be born again to see the kingdom of God. Evidently, Nicodemus took what Jesus said to mean another physical birth by entering again into his mother's womb, which was preposterous. Jesus admonished the learned Nicodemus for not knowing what the kingdom of God was all about.

Nicodemus kept an open mind and heart toward Jesus. Once, when the Pharisees sought to bring Jesus in for questioning, he even spoke up for Jesus, saying, "Our law does not judge people without first giving them a hearing to

find out what they are doing, does it?" (John 7:51).

After Jesus' death, Nicodemus became more bold in following him. Accompanying Joseph of Arimathea, Nicodemus brought about 75 pounds of spices to the tomb to anoint Jesus' body after Joseph received permission from Pilate to take the body for burial. Nicodemus assisted with burial preparations by helping Joseph wrap Jesus' body with the spices and strips of linen, in accordance with Jewish custom.

For further study, see John 3:2–9; 7:50–52; 19:38–42, 59.

❖

NOAH (NOH uh) *rest or comfort;* Genesis 5:29

The son of Lamech and the grandson of Methuselah, Noah appears in the tenth generation after Adam in the genealogies of Genesis. Singled out by God to preserve life on earth when all others proved undeserving, he became the center of one of the most familiar stories found in the Bible.

Noah and his family lived in a world so violent and so wicked that the Lord decided he would not allow humans to exist any longer. However, in the midst of this hedonism, there was one man—Noah—who had faith in God and lived a righteous and blameless life. God revealed to Noah his plan to destroy not only corrupt humanity but also the physical earth in its entirety by a deluge of water not yet known to humankind.

So righteous was Noah that God made a covenant with him, a promise of safety for him and his family, and a place of preservation for two of every kind of animal on the earth. In preparation for the floodwaters, the Lord gave Noah a 120–year project, telling him to build an ark of cypress wood coated with pitch inside and out. God gave him precise instructions and dimensions: It was to be 450 feet long, 75 feet wide, and 45 feet tall. Noah did everything just as God commanded.

> *Noah ... had faith in God and lived a righteous and blameless life.*

Noah was a little over 600 years old when God released the floodwaters and caused underground springs to burst open. Noah made the ark his home while the rains fell for 40 days and 40 nights on the entire earth. After 150 days, the waters had receded enough to reveal the mountaintops, and Noah's boat landed on the mountains of Ararat. After 40 days, Noah opened the only window in the ark and released a raven, which kept flying back. Noah then set free a dove from the window, but it also returned. Seven days later, Noah again sent out the dove, and finally it returned with an olive leaf in its mouth. Noah then knew that vegetation had begun to grow, and soon they would be able to leave the ark. Seven more days passed, and Noah again released the dove. Noah was assured that the earth was again habitable when the dove did not return.

After the rain water dried up on the earth, Noah removed the covering from the ark and saw the dry land. Almost two months later, the Lord told Noah and his family to leave the ark and liberate the animals. Noah, still obedient and faithful to God, stepped out of the ark with his family and built an altar, giving praise to God for his deliverance. God then promised to never again curse the earth or completely destroy it with water. As a sign of his pledge, God put a rainbow in the sky and promised to remember his covenant every time the colorful arc appeared.

For further study, see Genesis 5:28–32; 6:8—9:29; Matthew 24:38, 39; Hebrews 11:7; 1 Peter 3:20; 2 Peter 2:5.

❖

PAUL (PAWL) *little;* **1 century A.D.; Acts 7:58**

As Stephen, the first Christian martyr, was being stoned for his faith, Paul (also called Saul) watched in approval. That day sparked a great persecution against the church, scattering fearful Christians in Jerusalem throughout Judea and Samaria. At the head of this persecution was Paul, a Jew educated in Greek culture and born a Roman citizen. He made it his mission to utterly destroy the church, going from house to house and dragging Christian men and women to prison.

After Stephen's death, Paul threatened Christians with arrest and death for quite some time. He sought and received authority from the high priest to travel to Damascus and arrest Christians there. On his way to Damascus, however, he was surrounded by a bright light, which blinded him and knocked him to the ground. He heard a voice saying, "Saul, Saul, why do you persecute me? I am Jesus, whom you are persecuting" (Acts 9:4–5). Jesus then told him to go into the city where he would be told what to do. The blind Paul was led by his companions into Damascus, where a disciple named Ananias restored his sight. After spending several days with Jesus' disciples, Paul embraced the faith of the Christians he had been persecuting, and he began preaching about Jesus, astonishing his listeners with his sudden conversion.

After many days of powerful preaching in Damascus, the tables were turned and the Jews sought to kill him. Paul

Paul began preaching about Jesus, astonishing his listeners with his sudden conversion.

escaped by being lowered over the city walls in a basket and fleeing to Jerusalem, where he stayed with Peter for 15 days. Paul still received a suspicious reception from the other disciples until Barnabas interceded for him, relating the details of his conversion.

Later, Paul went on three momentous missionary journeys, and at the end of the third journey, Christians in Jerusalem warmly received him. However, when a group of Jews recognized him in the temple, they stirred up a huge crowd against him. Roman soldiers subsequently arrested him, protecting him from an angry mob. The commander ordered him whipped and questioned, but Paul's proof of Roman citizenship terminated any further actions by the troops, since it was illegal to flog a Roman citizen who had not been found guilty.

While Paul's enemies formed a conspiracy to kill him, the Romans secretly removed Paul from Jerusalem, taking him to Caesarea, where Governor Felix imprisoned him for two years. When Festus took over as governor, the conspirators tried to convince Festus to take Paul to Jerusalem, but Festus insisted that Paul be tried in Caesarea. Since King Agrippa had stopped by to pay his respects to the governor, Festus involved the king in the dispute over Paul. After hearing Paul's story, the king announced he could find nothing in Paul that deserved death or imprisonment.

Since Paul had appealed to Caesar, he was sent to Rome for judgment. In Rome, Paul was allowed to live by himself except for a soldier who guarded him. He stayed there two years and boldly preached about the kingdom of God to everyone who came to visit him, as well as to people in other provinces through letters he sent by emissaries.

The Bible does not record Paul's death, but in his last message to Timothy just prior to the traditional date of his death, Paul indicates that his end is near. The fourth-century church historian Eusebius records that Paul was taken to Rome and beheaded in Nero's persecution in A.D. 67.

For further study, see Acts, Romans, 1 Corinthians, 2 Corinthians, Galatians, Ephesians, Philippians, Colossians, 1 Thessalonians, 2 Thessalonians, 1 Timothy, 2 Timothy, Titus, Philemon.

❖

PETER (PEE tuhr) *rock;* A.D. 1 century; Matthew 4:18

Peter, called Simon, was a fisherman who became one of Jesus' first disciples. At times he exhibited unwavering faith, and yet at other times his faith was greatly shaken in the face of adversity. Although he had boldly declared his commitment to Jesus, later at one critical point he denied ever knowing him.

Peter first lived in Bethsaida but later resided in Capernaum, where Andrew, his brother, introduced him to Jesus. Andrew told Peter that he had found the Messiah. Upon meeting Peter, Jesus called him by name (Simon) and then changed his name to Peter. Little did Peter know that one day he would confess that Jesus was the Son of the living God and Jesus would call him the foundation of the church and the recipient of the keys to the kingdom of heaven.

Following these first events with Jesus, Peter was evidently with him constantly, observing his ministry firsthand. Though Peter saw his own mother-in-law healed by Jesus, it was as one of the inner circle of disciples closest to Jesus (along with James and John) that he really experienced the heart of Jesus' ministry. These three were the only ones invited to go with Jesus to the house of Jairus to see Jesus raise his daughter from the dead amidst the crying and wailing of the mourning family. These three men were the only ones taken up with Jesus on a high mountain to witness his transfiguration, where Jesus' face shone like the sun and his clothes became dazzling white. They witnessed the appearance of Moses and Elijah and heard them talk to Jesus. These same three disciples were also nearest to Jesus at the place of his greatest sorrow in the garden of Gethsemane.

Even though Peter steadfastly declared that he would lay down his life for Jesus, he ended up denying his association with Jesus completely. On the night of Jesus' arrest, Peter displayed his cowardice in the courtyard of Caiaphas when he denied three times that he was one of Jesus' disciples. Following his third denial, a rooster crowed, fulfilling Jesus' prediction at the Last Supper that Peter would deny him three times before the cock crowed twice. Peter wept bitterly.

Peter's failures, however, did not overshadow his faith or his passion. After receiving news that Jesus had risen from death, Peter ran to the tomb to see for himself. Peter was with Jesus several times while the Master remained on earth after his resurrection and before his ascension.

After receiving the Holy Spirit on Pentecost, the disciples began preaching in a variety of foreign tongues, which drew the attention of large crowds. Some were amazed by the disciples' display, but others questioned it, attributing it to drunkenness. Spurred by these accusations, Peter stood up and addressed the crowd in a loud voice, explaining what led to the events of Pentecost and telling the people to repent. His sermon was responsible for the conversion of about 3,000 people that day.

Peter . . . fought and won the battle to accept Gentiles into the church.

Peter continued to preach the gospel fearlessly, and one day while praying in the town of Joppa, he experienced a vision that would eventually take the church in a new direction. In this astounding vision the Lord instructed Peter to open the church to non-Jews. Although this policy would cause great controversy among Jewish believers, Peter, among others, fought and won the battle to accept Gentiles into the church.

Although the details of Peter's activities late in life are uncertain, he is credited with the authorship of two biblical epistles. While no sources document Peter's death, church tradition holds that he suffered martyrdom at the hands of the Roman Emperor Nero sometime in the middle of the first century A.D.

For further study, see Matthew 16–17, 26; Mark 8–9, 14; Luke 9, 22; John 13:31–38; 18:15–27; 21:15–23; Acts 1–5; 9–12; 15; 1 Peter; 2 Peter.

❖

PHILEMON (fy LEE muhn)
friendship; A.D. 1 century;
Philemon 1:1

Philemon was a house church leader in the Lycus valley near Ephesus, where he owned profitable land and slaves. One of his slaves, Onesimus, stole money from him and fled to Rome, where he met the apostle Paul and was converted to Christianity. A runaway slave, if caught, had to be returned to his former master, who could choose to either re-enslave him or kill him. Those who sheltered runaway slaves could also be held financially liable. Assuming Philemon would be unforgiving toward his runaway slave, Paul wrote a compassionate letter on behalf of Onesimus, asking Philemon to accept him as a brother in Christ and not as a slave.

For further study, see Philemon.

❖

PHILIP (FIL ip) *lover of horses;* A.D. 1 century; Acts 6:5

Philip did much to carry out Peter's mandate to open the church to Gentiles and to other people traditionally shut out of Jewish society. As one of the leaders of the early church in Jerusalem, he helped meet the material needs of the Greek-speaking widows in the community, extending the church's social services to non-Jews. As an evangelist working with the apostle Peter, Philip brought the gospel to the mixed-race Samaritans. On the road from Samaria, he encountered a royal eunuch from Ethiopia and led him to conversion; the eunuch returned to his homeland and spread the gospel there. In his later years, Philip raised and trained four

gifted daughters to prophecy and preach. Thus, Philip pushed the frontiers of evangelism, moving beyond his deacon's role and his parish to embrace a wide variety of people whom earlier evangelists had ignored.

For further study, see Acts 6:1–7; 8:1–13, 26–40; 21:8–9.

❖

PILATE (PY luht) *javelin carrier;* governed A.D. 26–36; Matthew 27:2

Pontius Pilate served as the fifth Roman governor of Judea. Controversy and incompetence marred his ten-year governorship. Although a supposed expert at compromise, he earned no respect or allegiance, for others easily manipulated and outmaneuvered him.

Although Rome occupied Judea, the Jews still maintained some autonomy in following their religious laws and customs. The Sanhedrin (the Jewish governing council) was still in place, although its actions were subordinate to the secular law of Rome. Tension frequently erupted when Roman interests came into conflict with Jewish religious practices, and Pilate typically mishandled these situations.

All four Gospels record Jesus' trial and conviction, but John gives the most insight into the particular role of Pilate. After the Sanhedrin had ruled that Jesus was guilty of blasphemy, they did not have the legal authority to put anyone to death, so they decided to bring him before Pilate with the capital charge of treason for claiming to be the King of the Jews. A large group hostile to Jesus ushered him to Pilate's palace early on the Friday morning before Passover. Pilate asked Jesus if he was the King of the Jews, and Jesus answered that he was indeed a king, but his kingdom was not of this world. Pilate saw no crime against Rome and ordered that the case be taken to the Judean ruler Herod Antipas.

Herod refused to get involved and merely made a fool of Jesus. Dressed in a purple robe and a crown of thorns, Jesus was beaten, whipped, mocked by the soldiers, and returned to Pilate. Three times Pilate tried to exonerate Jesus, wanting no part in his death. But an angry partisan crowd relentlessly shouted, "Crucify him! Crucify him!" Pilate went before them with a wash basin and publicly washed his hands, claiming, "I am innocent of this man's blood; see to it yourselves" (Matthew 27:24). He then handed Jesus over for crucifixion.

For further study, see Matthew 27; Mark 15; Luke 23; John 18–19.

❖

PRISCILLA (prih SIL uh) *meaning unknown;* **A.D. 1 century; Acts 18:2**

When Priscilla chose to wed Aquila, a former Jewish slave, she undoubtedly shocked her wealthy Roman family. Tentmakers by trade, Priscilla and Aquila took Paul on as a business partner. When Emperor Claudius forced all Jews to leave Rome, Priscilla and Aquila took their business and gospel ministry to Corinth and Ephesus. As a result, they helped start three churches: at Rome, Corinth, and Ephesus. Because Priscilla's name appears more often before Aquila's, some scholars feel she was the leader of their joint efforts.

For further study, see Acts 18:1–3, 18–28; Romans 16:3; 1 Corinthians 16:19; 2 Timothy 4:19.

❖

 **RACHEL (RAY chuhl)** *ewe;* **20 century B.C.; Genesis 29:6**

Jacob was sent to find his uncle Laban at the urging of his mother Rebekah, who wanted him to escape his brother Esau's anger and find a wife in her homeland. Once there, Jacob fell in love with Rachel the minute he laid eyes on her. She turned out to be Laban's daughter. He met her at a well where he stopped to ask directions and ended up helping her water her father's sheep.

After Jacob worked for his uncle for a month, Laban offered to pay him for his labors. However, Jacob told Laban that he would work seven more years for him if, in return, he could marry Rachel. When the seven years had passed, Laban deceived Jacob by sending his veiled daughter Leah to Jacob's bed instead. He justified his decision by saying it was the custom to give the older daughter in marriage first.

Laban consented to Jacob's marriage to Rachel if Jacob would serve him an additional seven years. Jacob agreed, marrying her and fulfilling his contract with Laban. Rachel was Jacob's favorite wife, for he loved her more than Leah. However, God allowed Leah to have many children, while Rachel bore only two sons, Joseph and Benjamin. Sadly, Rachel died giving birth to Benjamin and was buried on the way to Bethlehem.

> *Rahab ... is mentioned among the great heroes of the faith in Hebrews 11.*

While Leah demonstrated faith in the Lord during her travails, Rachel was attached to her household idols, which she secretly stole from her father when she, Jacob, Leah, and their children returned to Jacob's homeland.

For further study, see Genesis 29–30; 35:16–29; Jeremiah 31:15; Matthew 2:18.

❖

RAHAB (RAY hab) *broad;* 15 century B.C.; Joshua 2:1

When Joshua began his leadership of Israel, he sent spies into the Promised Land to survey the opposition. Two spies slipped into the city of Jericho and entered the home of Rahab, a prostitute, whose house was on the city wall.

When soldiers came looking for the spies, she hid the Israelites and told the soldiers that the two had left at nightfall. Like the other inhabitants of Jericho, Rahab had heard of the victories the Israelites had already won with the help of their God and of the miracle he had performed in parting the Red Sea to save them from the Egyptian army.

Convinced that the Israelite God was "indeed God in heaven above and on earth below," Rahab asked the spies to reward her for her assistance by sparing her and her family when the Israelites came to take Jericho. The spies promised her safety if she tied a scarlet cord in her window and had all her relatives in her house at the time of the attack. When the way was clear, she let the spies down by a rope through her window and warned them to hide in the hills for three days.

When the Israelites destroyed Jericho, they rescued Rahab and her family before setting fire to the city. She became the wife of Salmon and the mother of Boaz in the lineage of Jesus. She is mentioned among the great heroes of the faith in Hebrews 11.

For further study, see Joshua 2:2–21; 6:17–25; Matthew 1:5; Hebrews 11:31.

❖

REBEKAH (ruh BEK uh) *meaning unknown;* 21 century B.C.; Genesis 22:23

Rebekah was the daughter of Bethuel and the grandniece of Abraham, but she also became Abraham's daughter-in-law when she married his son Isaac. The aging Abraham had made his chief servant promise that he would find his son Isaac a wife, not among the Canaanites but among his own relatives in his own country. His servant was not to take Isaac with him to find a wife but was to rely upon an angel to show him who the willing woman would be. The servant, even as he was praying, found Rebekah, a courteous, kind woman who offered him water and gave him lodging with her family. She and her family agreed that she should travel to Canaan to marry Isaac.

When Rebekah and the servent arrived in Canaan, Isaac saw Rebekah coming, riding on a camel. She got down from her camel and went to him. They were married, but Rebekah remained barren for 20 years. Finally, after Isaac pleaded with the Lord, Rebekah bore twin sons, Jacob and Esau. The twins were in conflict even in the womb; Jacob was born clutching Esau's heel. The favoritism of Isaac for Esau and Rebekah for Jacob increased the brothers' strife. Rebekah, who overheard Isaac promising Esau his inheritance, was determined to obtain it for Jacob. She helped Jacob deceive the eld-

erly Isaac into granting him Esau's birthright.

When Rebekah died, she was buried in a tomb in a cave at Machpelah, the same place where Abraham, Sarah, and Isaac were buried.

For further study, see Genesis 24–27; 49:31; Romans 9:10.

❖

REUBEN (ROO ben) *behold a son;* 20 century B.C.; Genesis 29:32

The firstborn of Jacob's 12 sons, Reuben lived in a household rife with jealousy and bitterness. Being the oldest, he tried to save his half-brother's life, but the other brothers sold Joseph into slavery. Years later, Reuben offered his own two sons as hostages when Joseph exacted justice on his brothers.

Reuben lost favor with his father, however, by sleeping with Bilhah, one of his father's concubines. On his deathbed, Jacob used harsh words for his eldest son because of this trespass.

For further study, see Genesis 29:32; 30:14; 35:22–23; 37:1–36; 42:22–37; 46:8–9; 48:5; 49:3–4; Exodus 6:14; Numbers 1:20–21; 32:1–33; Deuteronomy 21:15–17; 33:6; 1 Chronicles 5:1.

❖

RUTH (ROOTH) *companion* or *friend;* 12 century B.C.; Ruth 1:4

A famine in Bethlehem forced the Hebrew family of Elimelech to go to Moab, where both of his sons married

Moabite women. His son Mahlon married a woman named Ruth. After Elimelech and his sons died, Naomi, Elimelech's wife, decided to return to Bethlehem. Naomi considered taking her daughters-in-law with her, but instead she told them to remain in Moab. Ruth, however, refused to leave Naomi.

Once in Bethlehem, Naomi convinced Ruth to work in the wheat fields. Boaz, the owner of the field, noticed Ruth and was drawn to her. He told his foreman to instruct the workers to secretly help her and protect her from attacks.

Under Israelite law, a dead man's nearest relative had the right to marry or "redeem" his widow. If that relative refused, that right would pass on to the nearest kin. Since Boaz was Mahlon's relative, he waited at the city gate for a closer relative to claim redemption rights to Ruth. One was willing to buy Mahlon's land but not to marry Ruth. The relative agreed that Boaz could marry Ruth and took off one sandal and handed it to Boaz to seal their arrangement. Ruth and Boaz were married and had a son named Obed, who had a son named Jesse, who became the father of David, Israel's most illustrious and loved king.

For further study, see Ruth.

❖

SAMSON (SAM suhn) *sun's man* or *distinguished;* 11 century B.C.; Judges 13:24

Manoah and his wife wanted a child, but his wife could not conceive until the Lord solved their infertility problem. An angel announced they would soon have a son: "It is he who shall begin to deliver Israel from the hand of the Philistines" (Judges 13:5). Israel and Philistia were neighbors, but the Philistines were the dominant power of the region, and their presence was a corrupting influence on the culture of Israel.

The angel also told Manoah that his son, Samson, would be bound to a Nazirite's vow. The Nazirites were a consecrated class of people who chose to set themselves apart for God's special use. The Nazirite's vow was one of abstinence and consecration. According to the law of Moses (Numbers 6:1–21), Nazirites had to abstain from alcohol or any drink made from grapes to symbolize their disdain for worldly culture. Nazirites also abstained from cutting their hair, touching dead bodies, and eating anything that the Mosaic law considered unclean.

Samson broke every rule set down for him as a Nazirite. His first breach was in marrying a non-Jewish Philistine woman and drinking wine at his wedding. Later, Samson touched the decaying carcass of a lion he had killed and ate honey from its innards.

Despite his rebellion, Samson proved an effective if unwitting tool of the Lord. When the impulsive Samson took the Philistine Delilah as his lover, he shared with her the secret of his super-human strength—his unshaven hair. When the Philistine lords found out his secret and shaved his head one night, yet another Nazirite vow was broken and his strength left him. Blinded and enslaved by the Philistines, he appealed to the power of God for vengeance. Because of his faith, his strength was restored, and Samson tore down a Philistine temple, killing himself and thousands of his enemies.

For further study, see Numbers 6; Judges 13–16; Hebrews 11:32–34.

❖

SAMUEL (SAM yoo uhl) *name of God* or *God hears;* 11 century B.C.; 1 Samuel 1:20

Elkanah and Hannah were a devout couple from Ramathaim zophim in the hill country of Ephraim. Hannah had long been childless, and on an annual pilgrimage to the shrine at Shiloh, she promised the Lord that if she was given a son, he would be consecrated to God's service.

In time, she gave birth to a child she called Samuel, because God had heard

Samson proved an effective if unwitting tool of God.

her. Hannah kept her promise and brought the toddler to Shiloh, formally dedicated him, and left him there to be reared by Eli the priest. As he grew, Samuel learned to help with the religious services, wearing a linen *ephod,* or priestly apron. Every year Hannah and Elkanah came to Shiloh to worship, and each time Hannah brought Samuel a robe she had made for him. The boy thrived in this environment, cared for by Eli and admired by the people who came to Shiloh.

One night, while Samuel was still a boy, God revealed himself to the lad. At first, Samuel thought he was hearing the voice of the aging high priest, and he went to him. Eli sent Samuel back to bed. The third time this happened, Eli told Samuel that it was the Lord calling and instructed Samuel in the way he should answer. When God spoke again, he told Samuel about the downfall of the house of Eli because of the corruption of Eli's two sons, the priests Hophni and Phinehas. The next morning Eli insisted that Samuel tell him what he had heard. When Samuel told him everything, it became clear that God had made Samuel a prophet, and news of this spread everywhere.

Later, Samuel's role as a prophet and a religious judge was established throughout the land. He settled in Ramah, close to Jerusalem, built an altar to the Lord, and administered justice to Israel.

Nevertheless, the Hebrew people wanted someone to rule over them like the kings of neighboring countries. Samuel felt rejected by their demand for a ruler, and he prayed about the matter. At God's bidding, the judge lectured the people about the evils of kingship, and what they could expect from the one who would reign over them. Undeterred by Samuel's words, the people insisted on having a king to govern them and lead them in battle. Samuel finally agreed to their demand. Sometime later, God revealed to Samuel that a young Benjaminite named Saul was the one selected to become the first king of Israel. So Samuel poured oil on Saul's head and anointed him ruler.

For a time, Saul depended on Samuel for God's instructions, but one time when the Philistines again threatened the Israelites, Saul, unable to wait for Samuel to come and make ritual sacrifices to the Lord before battle, performed the rituals himself. When Samuel arrived, he rebuked Saul for his actions and warned him that because of his disobedience, his kingship would not continue for long. He told Saul that the next king would be "a man after God's own heart" (1 Samuel 13:14).

> *It became clear that God had made Samuel a prophet, and news of this spread everywhere.*

Yet Saul disobeyed Samuel a second time. He went against God's order to execute King Agag by sparing Israel's notorious enemy. After this tragic breach, Samuel made no more official visits to see Saul. Samuel's next task was to visit Bethlehem and secretly anoint young David, the son of Jesse, as Israel's next king.

Samuel passed away while Saul was still king. The prophet was buried at Ramah, and all of Israel mourned him. In a strange incident after Samuel's death, Saul attempted to consult the spirit of Samuel for help, contacting him through an old witch of Endor. When Samuel's spirit appeared, Samuel rebuked the frightened king and sternly warned about the defeat of Israel and his impending death. The king fainted when he heard the news, and the next day the prediction came true.

For further study, see 1 Samuel 1–16; 19; 28; Psalm 99:6; Hebrews 11:32.

❖

SARAH (SAYR uh) *princess;* 22 century B.C.; Genesis 11:29

Sarah (first known as Sarai) was Abraham's half-sister on his father Terah's side, and she became Abraham's wife before the family left Ur of the Chaldees to make the journey to Haran. On their way, famine forced Sarah and her family to stop in Egypt. To avoid falling victim to the custom that one could kill a foreigner to take his wife, Abraham passed her off as his sister. Pharaoh brought Sarah into his household and gave her alleged brother lavish gifts. When Pharaoh's household became afflicted with plagues, he learned the truth about Sarah and Abraham. Upset by the deception, he returned Abraham's wife to him and told the Hebrew family to leave Egypt.

Sarah was childless—a situation made harder by the Lord's promise that Abraham's offspring would be a great nation. Finally, when Sarah was 90, the Lord told Abraham that she would bear a son. Sarah laughed when she heard this news, but in due time the child was born and named Isaac. Sarah died at the age of 127 and was buried beside Abraham in the family tomb at Hebron.

For further study, see Genesis 12–23; Isaiah 51:2.

❖

SAUL (SAHL) *asked;* ruled 1050–1010 B.C.; 1 Samuel 9:2

Saul came from a wealthy, influential family. He worked for his father, Kish, who was from the tribe of Benjamin, growing wheat and herding donkeys. Saul was at least a head taller than most men and extremely good looking.

One day, Saul was searching for his father's lost donkeys when he turned to the prophet Samuel for assistance and was given instead a most surprising decree. Pouring oil over the young man's head, Samuel revealed, "The Lord has anointed you ruler over his people Israel" (1 Samuel 10:1). Saul was reluctant to assume this new role of king; in fact, when his selection was announced to the people of Israel, he hid among the pack animals in the hope that he would be passed over.

The people delighted in Saul's first military victory—a surprise attack at night against the Ammonites. Saul went on to further military victories, and his popularity grew tremendously.

Despite his military campaigns, Saul's relations with Samuel were failing. As king, Saul made the military decisions, but Samuel, as priest, was responsible for overseeing the religious aspects of army life to ensure that Israel remained in God's favor. During one battle with the Philistines, after impatiently waiting seven days for Samuel to come and administer a burnt offering, Saul took religious affairs into his own hands by performing the sacrifice himself. Samuel rebuked Saul, warning him that for this sin, God would one day replace him with a new, more worthy king.

Saul again clashed with Samuel during the conquest of the Amalekites. Samuel had advised that holy retribution be wrought on these people and that they and their livestock be slaughtered. Saul took Agag, their king, captive, but then allowed the Amalekite troops to take sheep and cattle as plunder to offer as sacrifices to God. Samuel responded harshly. Once again Samuel told Saul that God would bring another to take his place. Saul begged for clemency but was refused. This was the last time that the two saw each other alive.

In the ensuing years, King Saul became increasingly distraught and unstable while he waited with dread for his kingdom to

> *As David's popularity grew, Saul became increasingly jealous and vengeful, and he eventually recognized David as the one who would replace him.*

be taken from him. His advisors sought a musician to soothe his torment. Ironically, the gifted young lyrist they chose was none other than the king-to-be, David. Saul showed great love for the lad, taking him in as his armor bearer, but as David's popularity grew, Saul became increasingly jealous and vengeful, and he eventually recognized David as the one who would replace him as king.

As Saul's hatred of David became more obvious, his kingship lost support, even within his own family. His son Jonathan, who had become close friends with David, refused to aid his father in his schemes. David ultimately had to flee, and Saul relentlessly pursued him throughout Israel. Twice David had the opportunity to slay Saul, but David refused to kill Israel's king.

When Israel faced a threat from the gathering Philistine army, Saul, in a desperate and misguided attempt to connect with God, turned to a sorceress from Endor, hoping to summon the spirit of Samuel, who had died. The prophet did appear to him and predicted imminent death for Saul and his family. In battle the next day, the Philistines slaughtered Saul's army. Wounded by an arrow, Saul himself begged his armor bearer to finish the job and kill him. When his servant refused, Saul fell on his own sword. The Philistines cut off Saul's head, stripped off his armor, and hung his body and those of his sons on a wall as carrion. Later, some Israelites retrieved the bodies and gave them a proper burial and respectful funeral.

For further study, see 1 Samuel 9–29; 31.

❖

SOLOMON (SAHL uh muhn)
peaceable; ruled 970–930 B.C.; 2 Samuel 12:24

Early in his reign, King Solomon was the wisest man of his era, a master of proverbial lore, and an insightful problem-solver. Despite his famed sagacity, however, he was often discouraged and was finally led astray by the religions of a number of pagan wives. Eventually his heart grew cold to God.

Solomon succeeded to the throne of Israel in an unprecedented manner: Unlike Saul or David, he did not have the triumphant military war record or the charismatic personality to be anointed king. Instead, Bathsheba, his mother and one of David's many wives, conspired to make him Israel's king. Although others were in line ahead of him for the monarchy, it was Solomon who succeeded to the throne. To solidify his hold on power, Solomon had his half-brother Adonijah killed.

Early in his reign, Solomon received a vision of God while performing a sacrifice. When God asked the young king what gift he wanted, Solomon asked for wisdom to "discern between good and evil" (1 Kings 3:9) so that he might be a better ruler of God's people. The request so pleased God that he also bestowed a blessing of wealth and prosperity on the king.

In time, Solomon had an astounding 700 wives and 300 concubines. Many of the marriages were calculated to foster internal political alliances or international relations, or to increase Solomon's world-famous wealth, and the great king's downfall is attributed to these pursuits. Although he clearly accomplished much in a material sense, he let go of the ways of God in pursuing these ends and brought strife upon the nation. To accommodate the demands of many of his foreign wives, Solomon freely allowed pagan worship in a variety of forms and so lost God's favor. In punishment, Solomon's peaceful reign was disrupted toward the end of his life by threats of violence from outside the nation. More importantly, the heavy burdens he placed on his people prompted the kingdom to be torn in two shortly after his death; ten of Israel's tribes broke away to form the northern kingdom, while only two, Judah and Benjamin, remained loyal to the house of David.

For further study, see 1 Kings 1–14; 1 Chronicles 28–29; 2 Chronicles 1–9.

❖

STEPHEN (STEE vuhn) *crown* or *crown-bearer;* A.D. 1 century; Acts 6:5

Acclaimed "a man full of faith and the Holy Spirit" (Acts 6:5), Stephen was chosen as one of the first seven deacons of the early Christian church. For his public arguments using Scripture to promote the spread of the gospel, Stephen was convicted of blasphemy by the Jewish high council and stoned to death, becoming the first Christian martyr. At his death Stephen commended his spirit to God and asked that his executioners be forgiven as Jesus had done on the cross.

For further study, see Acts 6–7.

❖

TABITHA (TAB i thuh) *gazelle*; A.D. 1 century; Acts 9:36

While Peter was in Lydda healing a paralytic named Aeneas, a woman named Tabitha (Dorcas in Greek) became ill and died in nearby Joppa. She was respected for doing good and helping the poor. The disciples sent two men to retrieve Peter, who, upon his arrival, was taken to an upstairs room where the body lay attended by mourners. Peter asked them to leave the room, and after they stepped out, he went down on his knees and prayed. He then told Tabitha to get up. She opened her eyes and sat up. Peter helped her to her feet and presented her to her people. News of this marvelous miracle spread quickly and prompted a great many people to accept the gospel.

For further study, see Acts 9:36–40.

❖

TAMAR (TAY mahr) *palm tree*; 19 century B.C.; Genesis 38:6

When Judah's wicked son Er died, leaving his widow Tamar childless, Judah gave his second son Onan to her so she could have a child. According to custom, a brother-in-law was obligated to provide his brother's childless widow with a child, but that child would be considered the heir and descendant of the deceased man. Unwilling to fulfill this duty, Onan spilled his semen on the ground when he lay with Tamar. His actions angered God, who put him to death. Judah then sent Tamar to live with her father until the time that his youngest son, Shelah, would be old enough to give her a son. Fearing that Shelah would die as his brothers had, Judah never sent him to fulfill this familial obligation.

Meanwhile, Tamar realized that Judah had been dishonest with her, so after learning that he would be traveling to Timnah, she covered her face with a veil and posed as a prostitute at a point on Judah's route. Not recognizing her as his daughter-in-law, he solicited her. Tamar agreed to sleep with him but requested he leave his signet, cord, and staff as collateral. When Judah later sent a friend with his payment, Tamar was nowhere to be found. Some months later, Judah learned that Tamar had become pregnant, and he angrily ordered her burned to death for her impropriety. As she was being led to the fire, Tamar produced Judah's signet, cord, and staff. Recognizing them, Judah rescinded her death sentence. Tamar gave birth to twin boys, Perez and Zerah. Perez became an ancestor of David and Jesus.

For further study, see Genesis 38; Ruth 4:12; 1 Chronicles 2:4; Matthew 1:3.

❖

TIMOTHY (**TIM uh thee**) *man who honors God;* A.D. 1 century; Acts 16:1

Timothy became one of Paul's chief associates and the eventual bishop of Ephesus. Born to a pagan Greek father and a pious Jewish mother, Timothy was raised as a Jew and converted to Christianity when Paul visited his hometown of Lystra. Paul became Timothy's father in the faith and his mentor for missionary work. Paul selected Timothy as his associate because of his bicultural background and the respect accorded him by the people at Lystra and Iconium. In joining Paul's second missionary journey, Timothy had to submit to painful adult circumcision and imprisonment in Roman jails.

Young Timothy was placed in charge of certain projects at the church in Ephesus. Apparently due to his youth, however, he was not respected by some Christians. Timothy also suffered bouts of ill health and moments of anxiety. Hence, some considered his mission there a failure. Nor surprisingly, when Timothy was at Corinth, Paul wrote a letter to the Corinthian Christians, warning them to go easy on his young friend.

Despite his reputation for being timid and sickly, Timothy proved to be sensitive, affectionate, and loyal. Paul and the church elders imparted on Timothy a special endowment for ministry that would help him persevere during hard times.

For further study, see Acts 16:1–5, 16–40; 17:14; 18:5; 19:22; 20:4–5; Romans 16:21; 1 Corinthians 4:14–17; 16:10–11; 2 Corinthians 1:18–20; Philippians 2:19–24; 1 and 2 Timothy.

❖